# KeyBytes®
## for Teachers

An Interactive Course in ICT

**Editorial team:**

**Marilyn Leask**
De Montfort University, Bedford

**Lyn Dawes**
BECTa

**David Litchfield**
Brierton School, Hartlepool

**SUMMERFIELD PUBLISHING LIMITED**

*KeyBytes*® for Teachers

First published in 2000 by
Summerfield Publishing Ltd
PO Box 16
Evesham
WR11 6WN
Great Britain

Text and artwork copyright © Summerfield Publishing Ltd 2000

All rights reserved. No part of this book, including interior design, cover design, and icons, may be reproduced or transmitted in any form, by any means (electronic, photocopying, recording, or otherwise) without the prior written permission of the publisher or under licence from the Copyright Licensing Agency Limited. Further details of such licences (for reprographic reproduction) may be obtained from the Copyright Licensing Agency Limited, of 90 Tottenham Court Road, London W1P 0LP.
The right of Marilyn Leask, Lyn Dawes and David Litchfield to be identified as authors of this work has been asserted by them in accordance with the Copyright, Designs and Patents Act 1988.

00   01   02   03   04 / 5   4   3   2   1

A catalogue record for this book is available from the British Library.

ISBN   1-901-995-11-9

**Trademarks:**
*KeyBytes* is a registered trademark under exclusive licence to Summerfield Publishing Ltd from Summerfield Business Services Ltd.

*Windows 3.11*, *Windows 95*, *Windows 98*, *Windows 2000* and *Windows NT* are registered trademarks of Microsoft Corporation. All other brand names and product names used in this book are trademarks, registered trademarks, or trade names of their respective holders.

Limit of Liability/Disclaimer of Warranty: The authors and publishers have used their best efforts to ensure accuracy in this book suitable to the usage expected. However Summerfield Publishing and the authors make no representation or warranties with respect to the accuracy or completeness of the contents of this book and specifically disclaim any implied warranties of merchantability or fitness for any particular purpose and shall in no event be liable for any loss of profit or any other commercial damage, including but not limited to special, incidental, consequential, or other damages.

Typeset by David Onyett, Publishing & Production Services, Cheltenham.
Printed and bound in China by Dah Hua Printing Press Co. Ltd.

# Contents

| | Preface | v |
|---|---|---|
| | Using the KeyBytes for Teachers Program | vi |
| Unit A | **Introducing KeyBytes** <br> A first introduction to computers and to *KeyBytes* | 1 |
| Unit B | **The Keyboard and Mouse** <br> A full hands-on tour using the keyboard and the mouse | 9 |
| Unit C | **Practice Makes Perfect** <br> A touch typing course followed by games to increase typing speed and accuracy | 17 |
| Unit D | **Hardware Basics** <br> Understanding what's going on – why, where and how! | 20 |
| Unit E | **Screen Technology** <br> From CRT to electronic whiteboards and virtual reality | 31 |
| Unit F | **Peripherals** <br> Getting optimum use from computer systems | 40 |
| Unit G | **Working with Windows** <br> All the core Windows skills learnt and practised | 51 |
| Unit H | **Word Processing** <br> Hands-on practice with all the main word processing functions | 63 |
| Unit I | **Spreadsheets** <br> Guided hands-on learning to become proficient in all the most-used spreadsheet functions | 76 |
| Unit J | **Databases** <br> Using, maintaining and setting up databases for a purpose | 89 |

Contents

| | | |
|---|---|---:|
| Unit K | **Graphics**<br>Drawing skills developed; plus<br>CAD/CAM explored | 98 |
| Unit L | **Publishing Your Work**<br>Design for differing target audiences<br>– and publishing on paper or on screen | 108 |
| Unit M | **Computers Doing the Work**<br>Enjoy simple programming problems and explore<br>where these can lead | 121 |
| Unit N | **Computers in Daily Life**<br>Consider how widespread the use of computers<br>is in our daily lives | 132 |
| Unit O | **Communications**<br>Step-by-step hand-holding through networks,<br>e-mail, intranets and the Internet | 143 |
| | **Using e-mail and the Internet<br>in Your Teaching**<br>Ideas for lesson planning and doing e-mail<br>and Internet projects | 161 |
| | **KeyBytes Final Test**<br>Where we find out what has been learnt<br>from the course | 172 |
| | **Self Assessment to Create Your<br>Personal Action Plan**<br>What are you going to do next? | 173 |
| | **Index** | 182 |
| | **Acknowledgements** | 183 |

# *Preface*

*KeyBytes* will teach you the core knowledge and skills you need to understand and use Information and Communication Technology intelligently and appropriately in your classroom and for other professional purposes.

Even if you've hardly ever used a computer, the hands-on tasks set, and the skills taught, soon will enable you to become quite expert.

If you're already 'a bit of a computer whizz' then you'll probably work through the first few *KeyBytes* units quite quickly: but there is still much to be learnt. When you have completed *KeyBytes* you'll be able to try some of the classroom projects mentioned on pages 161–167.

Throughout *KeyBytes* there's lots of hands-on practice, short checkpoints and frequent tests to keep you on your toes! *KeyBytes* tells you when to read the Coursebook and when to work on screen. By doing both things carefully you will maximise your learning.

After the main on-screen work in every *KeyBytes* unit is a 20 question test. *KeyBytes* marks each of these tests and makes a record of the results. When each end-of-unit test has been completed you will be prompted to try the Tasks in this Coursebook.

After the main units is a Coursebook-only unit on using e-mail and the Internet in your teaching.

Next you should return to the Program for the opportunity to have all your ICT knowledge and understanding examined in the *KeyBytes Final Test*. Once you finish this the Program calculates your final result and prints your Diploma.

The last part of *KeyBytes for Teachers* Coursebook tells you about assessing yourself and guides you to create your Personal Action Plan for the future. Try this on screen and print it out to remind you what you want to achieve.

You can work on *KeyBytes* on your own – or with a partner at the same screen. If you work with a partner then we suggest you **work together.** Work at a speed that suits you both. Discuss all the answers before giving the one you think is right.

One of the most important things though is to *enjoy KeyBytes*.

Good Luck!

# Using the KeyBytes for Teachers Program

The underlying Program for *KeyBytes for Teachers* has many sophisticated features. All of these are available to ICT trainers who use the full networked version; a few can be made accessible to individual users who have purchased the single-user version. One situation where individuals may want to make changes is if *KeyBytes* is being used on a particularly old or slow PC: then the 'speed' settings on *KeyBytes* may need adjustment.

Your ICT trainer has details of how to make adjustments. Alternatively contact the publishers of *KeyBytes* who can also give advice.

### General Rules for the use of *KeyBytes*!

**If you get stuck!** The panel at the foot of every *KeyBytes* screen gives instructions related to that screen. The Program demands a correct (or nearly correct) response before it will move forward to the next screen. If a mistake is made then the Program tries to work out what you have done wrong – and then gives further advice. It can't always work out exactly what has been done wrong – so read the instruction again carefully and try something different.

The notes in the chronology information (on your Program disk or available from your trainer) will help you overcome any remaining problems.

**Missing Word Exercises:** Where there is more than one acceptable answer to a Missing Word question then the Program will accept up to three choices of word. However, if you are having great difficulty in finding the required word then read the associated material in this Coursebook again. The word you need will always be found here. Each section of reading referred to in the Program is identified in this Coursebook with this icon:

**Passwords:** Each Unit of the Program is built up in sections. There are varying numbers of screens within each section – some sections take only two or three minutes to complete – others maybe 5 or 10 minutes (and one as much as 20 minutes). Whenever you exit from the Program in mid-section the password relating to that section is shown on the screen and you are asked to note it down. Each password is alphanumeric: the unit

*Using the KeyBytes for Teachers Program*

letter followed by a number. Next time you work with the Program you should enter at the password previously given – and then carry on from the point where you left off. The first password in each unit is shown below. See also the 'If you get stuck!' note above and the notes in the chronology information (on your Program disk or available from your trainer).

## Passwords to get you started in each unit:

| Unit A | A1 |
| Unit B | B1 |
| Unit C | C1 |
| Unit D | D1 |
| Unit E | E1 |
| Unit F | F1 |
| Unit G | G1 |
| Unit H | H1 |
| Unit I | I1 |
| Unit J | J1 |
| Unit K | K1 |
| Unit L | L1 |
| Unit M | M1 |
| Unit N | N1 |
| Unit O | O1 |

# Unit A
# *Introducing KeyBytes*

## INTRODUCTION

*KeyBytes* is a course that will teach you about Information and Communication Technology. Within each unit you will have the chance to practise what you have learned and check that you have understood each step.

Unit A introduces you to *KeyBytes* and provides you with the opportunity to check how much you already know. If you are being newly introduced to the use of a computer you will also learn and practise new skills.

The *KeyBytes* program contains prompts that tell you when to refer to this book. Whenever you stop working with the *KeyBytes* program, a password appears on screen. A list of passwords is supplied on the previous pages. When you wish to restart the program, you will be prompted by the program to type this password in order to start in the right place.

While working with the program, you will see two buttons at the bottom right of the screen. When buttons like this are 'active', you can see a dark grey box on them. Active buttons can be 'pressed' by using the mouse to 'point and click', or by using the Enter key on the keyboard.

Click on the Continue button to go on.

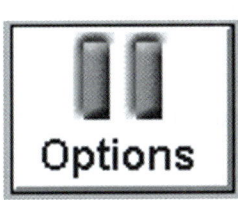
Click on the Options button and you get a choice.

Using the Enter key makes an 'active' button work.

Unit A: *Introducing KeyBytes*

## *Objectives*

In this unit you are introduced to:

- terms describing different parts of the computer systems.
- some important keys on the keyboard.
- the mouse.

**Key words**

**Program**  The program provides instructions for the computer. Without a program, a computer is just a useless box. KeyBytes is a ***program***.

**Button**  An area on the screen that can be made 'active' by the Tab key, Screen Cursor keys or mouse. Once 'active' it can be 'pressed' by using the Enter key or clicking the mouse button while the pointer is on the button.

> Continue with the computer

## THE MAIN PARTS

A computer consists of several main parts.

### The screen

Information and instructions are given to you on the screen. Other terms for the screen are:

> Monitor
> VDU (or visual display unit)

### The base unit

The computer's 'thinking and processing work' is done in the base unit. Other terms used to describe the base unit include:

> Case
> CPU (or central processing unit)
> Tower

The disk drives are inside the base unit. The base unit also houses the processor. The type of processor (Pentium III, 450 MHz, etc.) determines whether your computer is powerful enough to run the programs you want. Unit D provides further information.

### The keyboard

You can give instructions to the computer by using the keyboard or, for certain actions, the mouse.

### The mouse

The mouse also gives instructions to the computer.

### The hard disk drive

The hard disk drive stores the software used to run the programs and the information (data) passed to it by the processor. It passes that data back when it is asked for it by the program and the processor. It works at a very fast speed and only fails to work properly on rare occasions (which is why 'backing up' or keeping copies of your computer programs and files is so important). Important program data is always stored on a computer's hard disk because the hard disk is fast and reliable. Unit D provides further information.

### The floppy disk drive

This is usually found on the front of the base unit. It has a 9 cm (3.5 inches) wide opening that's covered by a flap. Because of its size the 'floppy disk drive' is sometimes called the 'three-and-a-half inch drive'.

### The CD-ROM disk drive

This too is usually housed in the base unit. A CD-ROM disk drive works much faster than a floppy disk and can hold large amounts of data. (It is possible to make your own CD-ROMs using a piece of equipment called a CD-ROM writer. These are not very expensive and CD-ROMs are cheap to make once you have the material, e.g. photographs and text from a school drama production.) Some people like to play their music CDs on this disk drive while they are working on their computers. Unit D provides further information.

### The speakers

Your computer might have two speakers that can be easily seen. On new machines the speakers are often integrated into the screen casing. You need speakers in order for you to be able to listen to CD-ROMs using speech (e.g. CD-ROMs for infants who are not yet reading) or music, or to access sound on the Internet (e.g. foreign language radio stations). On older machines there is often just one tiny speaker in the base unit. These tiny speakers have a more limited use.

Unit A: Introducing KeyBytes

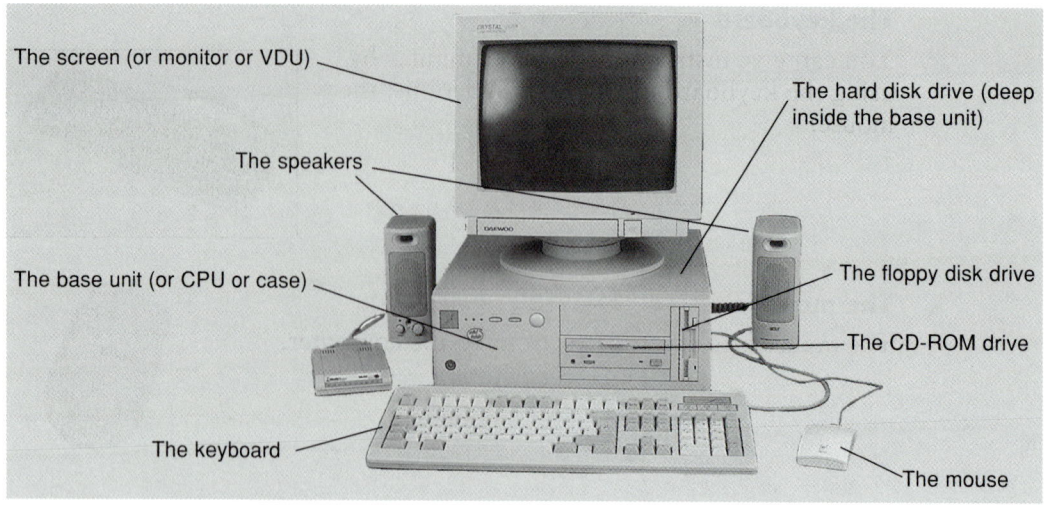

The screen (or monitor or VDU)
The hard disk drive (deep inside the base unit)
The speakers
The base unit (or CPU or case)
The floppy disk drive
The CD-ROM drive
The keyboard
The mouse

### The 'hardware' and 'software'

'Hardware' is a collective word for the main parts that make up a 'computer system'. The term 'software' refers to the programs.

```
Continue with the computer
```

## THE KEYBOARD – NOT THE MOUSE

### Aspects of the keyboard

More information about the keyboard is provided in Unit B. For Unit A, you need to be sure you know all about the mouse and enough about the keyboard to move around the *KeyBytes* program quickly.

### The Enter key

Sometimes the Enter key can be used to select something more quickly than using the mouse. The clue to knowing if the Enter key can be used is shown on the screen. If the button you want to 'press' has a dark grey box on it, or round it, this means that it is 'active' and that using the Enter key will activate it.

### The Tab key and the Screen Cursor keys

Often there are many buttons on the screen, but only one will have a dark grey box on it, or round it. Only that particular button is active. You can use the Tab key or the Screen Cursor keys to 'jump' from one button to another. Every time you press one of these keys, the 'box' will jump to another button on the screen. You can then use the Enter key to 'press' that button. When completing on-screen forms or filling in on-screen boxes you can use the Tab key to move from box to box.

Unit A: *Introducing KeyBytes*

 Jump between buttons with the Tab key ...

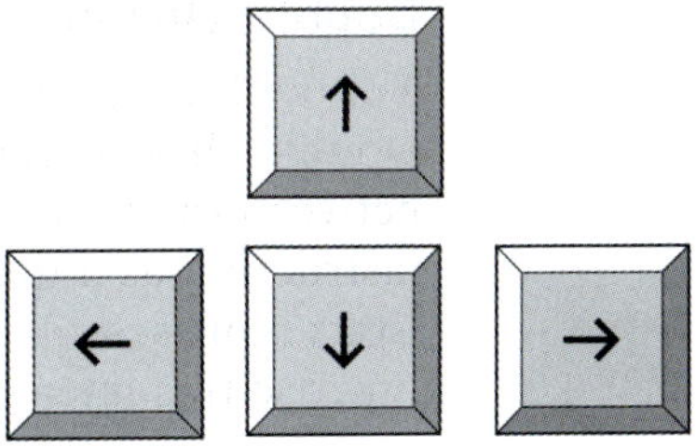

... or with the Screen Cursor keys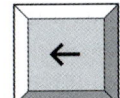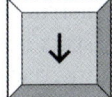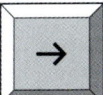

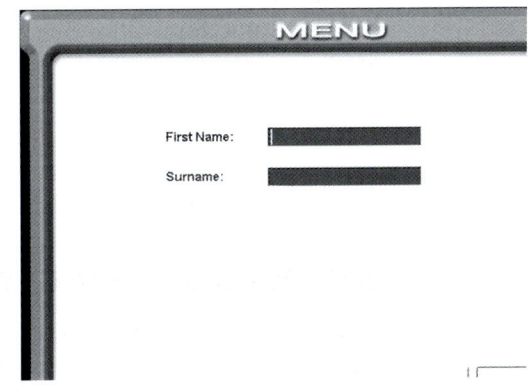

Jump from one line to another with the Tab key.

Also use the Tab key or the Screen Cursor keys to jump from one button to another.

Continue with the computer

## THE MOUSE

The mouse has two or three buttons. For most of *KeyBytes* you will only need the *left* button. Except where the program instructs you, the *right* button is not needed in *KeyBytes*.

The most comfortable way to use the mouse is to hold it flat on the desk under your cupped hand. Without putting any pressure on the mouse, guide it around the desk (or mousepad) with the tips of your fingers, using small, delicate movements. Keep the base of your hand on the desk. Keep a finger – usually the index finger – over the left button.

As you guide the mouse around the desk, watch the pointer on the screen. It will move in response to the mouse movements. When the pointer is over an item you want to select, quickly press and let go of the left button. You will hear a click. This is called 'point and click'.

5

Unit A: *Introducing KeyBytes*

### Double-clicking

You will not be surprised to learn that clicking twice is a double-click! Double-clicking must be done quickly. If you leave too much time between the first and second clicks, the computer does not register the instruction as a double-click. Double-clicking is used when you want to 'start a program', or 'open a file'. You will get the opportunity to practise this later in *KeyBytes*.

### Dragging

Moving something over the screen with the mouse is called dragging. To drag:

- Point
- Press and hold the mouse left button
- Drag to the position you want
- Let go of the mouse button

### BABBAGE'S DIFFERENCE ENGINE

In 1792 Charles Babbage was born near Teignmouth, in Devon, England. He studied mathematics at Cambridge University. He had the idea of building a calculating machine, which he thought would save time and be very accurate. He worked on the machine for 37 years and died in 1871 without ever finishing it. A part of the machine is on display in the Science Museum in London. Babbage had in fact thought up 'the computer', which is why Charles Babbage is called 'the father of the computer'.

A small part of Charles Babbage's Difference Engine

> Continue with the computer

# SUMMARY SUMMARY SUMMARY SUMMARY SUMMARY

- The computer shows information on the screen (or 'monitor' or 'VDU').
- The computer's thinking work is done in the base unit (or 'case' or 'CPU' or 'tower').
- You can give the computer instructions by using the keyboard and the mouse.
- The CD-ROM and floppy disk drives are usually in the front of the base unit.
- The floppy disk drive is also called the three-and-a-half inch disk drive.
- The hard disk drive stores the software used to run the programs and all the data (information) needed by the processor.
- The hard disk drive is inside the base unit.
- The word 'hardware' is used to encompass all the main parts of a computer; 'software' is used to describe the programs.
- If an on-screen button has a dark grey box on it, or round it, it is active.
- The Enter key can be used to press an on-screen active button.
- The Tab key lets you jump from one button on the screen to another.
- The Screen Cursor keys also let you jump from button to button.
- When you point with the mouse, then click the mouse button, this is called point and click.
- Usually the left mouse button will be the one to use in *KeyBytes*.
- Pointing and clicking twice quickly is called a double-click.
- Moving something over the screen with the mouse is called dragging.
- Charles Babbage had the idea for a computer about 175 years ago.

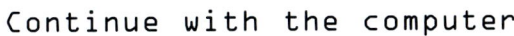
Continue with the computer

Unit A: *Introducing KeyBytes*

**TASKS**

1. Check that you know the names and the functions of the parts of the computer system that you are using and others around the school that are available to you.

2. Find out which computers have CD-ROMs and speakers and ask colleagues what they use them for.

3. Try to get access to a laptop if you haven't got one. Find out from your colleagues the advantages and disadvantages of laptops over desktops.

# Unit B

# The Keyboard and Mouse

## INTRODUCTION

The keyboard and mouse are used for data entry or input. In other words you can give instructions to the computer and you can enter information by using the keyboard and the mouse. This unit describes the use and functions of many of the special keys found on a computer keyboard. It also explains some of the uses of the mouse.

## Objectives

The objective of this chapter is to increase your familiarity with the layout and functions of the keyboard and mouse so that you can use them effectively in your work.

By the end of this unit you will:

- be more familiar with the layout of the keys on the keyboard.
- know the use and function of most of the keys.
- know how to use the keys and mouse to carry out some tasks.
- have had the opportunities to improve your keyboard skills.

**Key words**

| | | |
|---|---|---|
| | Character | A character can be:<br>Letters – like a b c d e f g etc, or<br>Capital letters – like A B C D E F G etc, or<br>Punctuation – like ! , ? ; . : ' etc, or<br>Signs – like + = – % etc, or<br>Symbols – like # $ & * @ etc. |
| | Text cursor | The flashing symbol that indicates your current position on screen. |
| | Function keys | The row of keys found along the top of the keyboard. These have different uses in different programs. |

Unit B: *The Keyboard and Mouse*

Help screen  An on-screen panel of information which tells you what can be done next. In many programs you find this screen if you press F1.

Numeric  This is information that consists of numbers only, e.g. a list with the age of every person in a school or college class.

```
Continue with the computer
```

## THE KEYBOARD LAYOUT

Information is mainly given to the computer by using the keyboard, so it is important that you become familiar with its layout and use. There are other layouts, but the one we will concentrate on is the usual 'qwerty' keyboard, so called because of the arrangement of the first six letters at the top left of the keyboard. Most full-sized keyboards have just over 100 keys.

The text cursor shows where on the screen the typed letters will appear.

The qwerty keyboard consists of four different areas.

**The areas on the keyboard**

1. Main keyboard area
2. Screen Cursor keys
3. Numeric keypad
4. Function keys

1. Main keyboard: this is used to type letters, numbers and punctuation.

2. Screen cursor keys: these are used to move the text cursor left, right, up and down and they are also used to jump from one button to another on screen.

3. Numeric keypad: this is used to type in lists of numbers.

4. Function keys: these are used to do different things in different programs, although there are certain conventions used in nearly all programs, e.g. F1 = Help.

Unit B: *The Keyboard and Mouse*

*Use the main keyboard area to type characters.*

*The numeric keypad is useful for number work.*

There are alternative layouts to the qwerty keyboards.

| This is the AZERTY layout used in France | This is the Dvorak layout devised in the 1920s and 30s for high productivity and ease of learning |

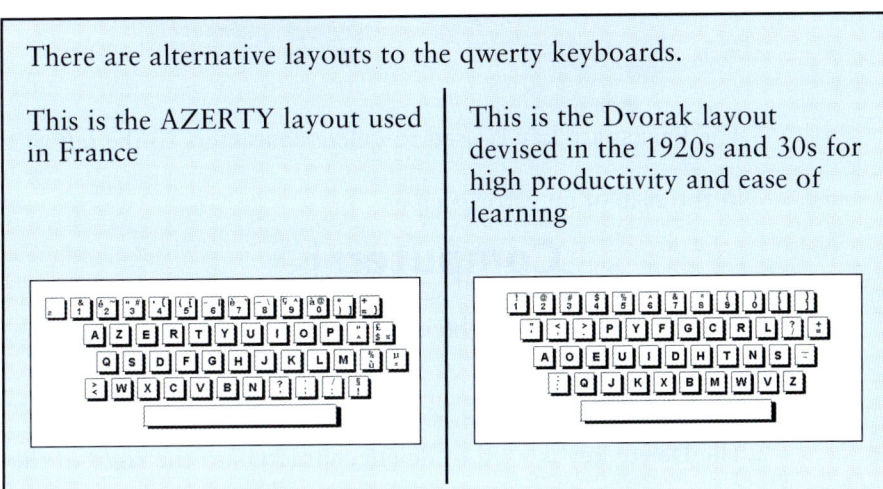

### A first look at the text cursor

The text cursor is a flashing symbol on the screen: often a vertical or horizontal line, or a block. It indicates where the next character that you type will appear. There are two ways to move the text cursor to a different position on the screen: you can use the cursor keys; or you can use the mouse pointer to point to where you want the text cursor, and click.

## Curso|

There are two ways to move the text cursor:

*Move the text cursor with the Screen Cursor keys:*

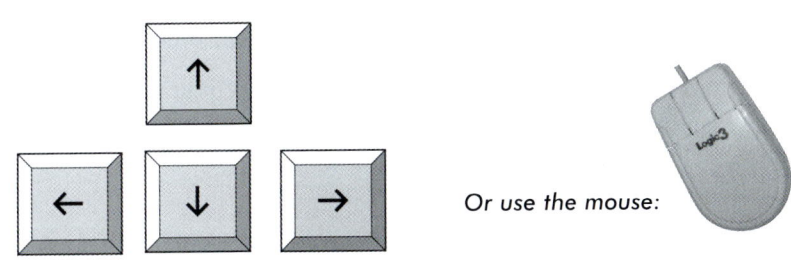

*Or use the mouse:*

Point at the place where you want the text cursor, then click.

11

Unit B: *The Keyboard and Mouse*

```
Continue with the computer
```

### SPACE BAR, BACKSPACE AND DELETE KEYS

The Space Bar is used to make spaces between the words.

The Backspace key is used to delete characters to the *left* of the cursor.

In the case of an error such as

# Computerr|

the Backspace key can be used to delete the final letter.

The Delete key is used to delete characters to the *right* of the cursor.

In the case of an error such as

# Comp|outer

the Delete key can be used. Position the text cursor to the left of the wrong character, and press Delete.

```
Continue with the computer
```

### SHIFT KEY AND CAPS LOCK KEY

Holding down the Shift key will allow you to type letters as capitals. It also allows you to type the upper character on keys where more than one character appears, e.g. *8, ?/, etc.

Unit B: *The Keyboard and Mouse*

The Caps Lock key works like a switch, 'locking' capital letters on when you press it once. To revert to lower case, press Caps Lock a second time. An indicator light on most keyboards reminds you when Caps Lock is on. Many word-processing programs, e.g. Word for Windows, have a facility to let you change the text to lower case if you inadvertently type for much longer than you meant to with the Caps Lock on. Unit H provides advice about how to do this.

    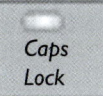

```
Continue with the computer
```

## MORE ABOUT THE CURSORS

### Mouse cursor

This moves around the screen in response to movements you make with the mouse. Most of the time and in most programs, the mouse cursor is shaped like an arrow. However it changes shape to indicate different functions:

- An arrow helps to locate the mouse cursor accurately when clicking buttons and moving lines in tables.

- An eggtimer or clock tells you that the computer is 'busy'. It will not accept more input until its task is complete.

- A thin 'I' shape is used to allow you to position the mouse cursor between characters in text passages. (Once the 'I' shape cursor is in the position you want, click the mouse! The 'I' shape mouse cursor changes into a text cursor.)

The pointer, the egg timer and the 'thin I' all show the position of the mouse on the screen. They are the 'mouse cursors'.

### A further look at the text cursor

The text cursor is the 'flashing line' cursor we used in the Backspace and Delete key exercises. As you type each new character the text cursor moves forward along the text line so it always indicates where the next character will be positioned. You can move the text cursor using the Screen Cursor keys or the mouse.

Unit B: *The Keyboard and Mouse*

### Screen Cursor keys

These have more than one use. You can use the Screen Cursor keys to move the text cursor left, right, up or down. Each press of the key moves the text cursor one character at a time. The Screen Cursor keys can also be used like the Tab key to move from one 'button' to another.

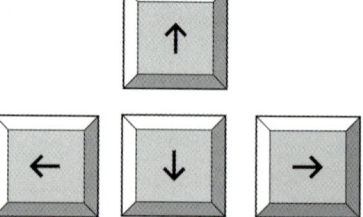

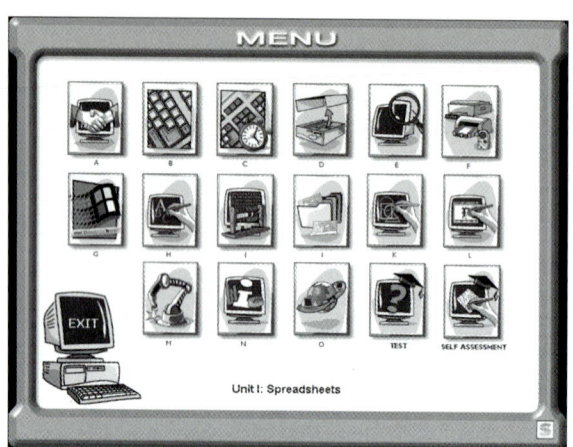

When you started KeyBytes one of the screens showed the KeyBytes menu. This menu has one button for each KeyBytes unit. With the mouse you pointed and clicked on Unit B. Next time you start a KeyBytes unit try using the Screen Cursor keys or the Tab key to move from button to button.

```
Continue with the computer
```

### THE FUNCTION KEYS

The Function keys are usually situated along the top of the keyboard, and are numbered F1, F2 and so on. There are certain conventions for the use of Functions keys – in many programs, pressing F1 will put the help menu on the screen – but mostly their functions are different from program to program. The literature included with the computer software details the use of the Function keys specific to the program. They are often 'short cut' keys: used to allow users to speedily perform often-used functions within the program.

```
Continue with the computer
```

Unit B: *The Keyboard and Mouse*

 **ESCAPE, CTRL AND ALT KEYS**

The Escape key is usually at the top left hand side of the keyboard and is labelled Esc. It is nearly always used to signal that you wish to cancel the last operation. That is, if you click a button by mistake, or change your mind once you have called up a menu, pressing Esc may cancel that instruction.

The Ctrl (short for Control) and Alt (short for alternate) keys are used to carry out various functions in conjunction with other keys. Both keys act like special shift keys, and are used in conjunction with a letter or another key pressed at the same time. You will use the Alt and Ctrl keys later in *KeyBytes*.

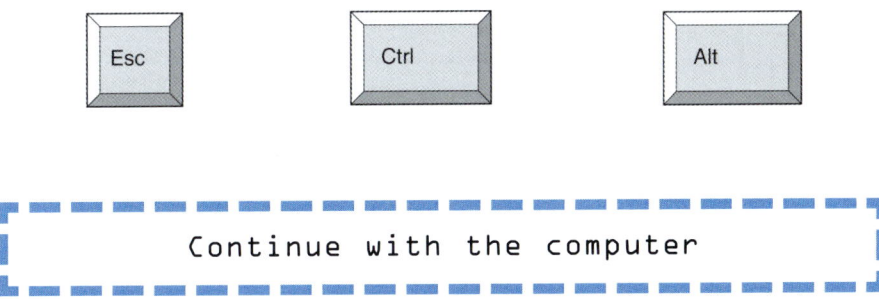

```
Continue with the computer
```

## SUMMARY SUMMARY SUMMARY SUMMARY SUMMARY

- The keyboard is used to enter data into the computer.
- It is used to type letters, numbers, symbols and commands.
- The Screen Cursor keys move the text cursor up and down, left and right.
- You can also move the text cursor using the mouse.
- Every letter, punctuation mark, symbol and sign is a character.
- The Backspace key deletes the character to the left of the text cursor.
- The Delete key removes characters to the right of the text cursor.
- The Shift key is used to type capital letters and the top characters on all the other keys (punctuation marks, symbols, signs, etc.).
- Use either the Screen Cursor keys or the mouse or the Tab key to jump from button to button on the screen.
- Pressing the F1 Function key usually gives you a Help screen.

Unit B: *The Keyboard and Mouse*

## SUM

- Other Function keys often have a different purpose in each different program.
- The Ctrl and Alt keys are used in conjuction with other keys for a variety of functions.

**TASK**

1. Review the keys again to ensure that you know how they function. Familiarity with the keyboard will enable you to produce documents with a professional look. Unit H provides further practice.

```
Continue with the computer
```

# Unit C
## Practice Makes Perfect

### INTRODUCTION

In Unit B you used the whole of the keyboard, but although you know what each key does, it will still probably take you a while to begin to type with any fluency.

This unit will begin to solve that problem. You will get lots of practice with the keyboard and your typing will become faster and more accurate.

### *Objective*

By the end of this unit you will have had a chance to improve your keyboarding skills.

Make a record of your results as you work through the unit.

Unit C is in two parts:

- A touch typing course.
- A typing tester.

The touch typing course teaches the best way to type. Once you can do it properly, your typing will become accurate and fast.

Learning to type is like riding a bike! It starts out being difficult, but once you get going it becomes much easier. Soon you will be able to do it without thinking.

In between rounds of the touch typing course, a practice game called Flying Words is provided. This will help you to increase your speed and accuracy.

In the second part of Unit C is the typing tester. This exercise will help you to find each key quickly. *KeyBytes* makes a record of your speed and notes whether you type the correct key or not. As you move through the exercises you will get quicker, but the exercises will get harder as well.

Unit C: *Practice Makes Perfect*

To touch type, you need to learn which finger to use for each key. The program uses a 'colour coding' system to allow for clear and brief instructions: you may want to put a felt-tip dot on each of your fingers!

The final round of the typing tester is more important than the others. The results of that round go into your end-of-unit test results.

In this second part of the unit, you will play another typing game called Plunge.

```
Continue with the computer
```

### DID YOU KNOW ...

The keys on the keyboards of the early mechanical typewriters were originally laid out in alphabetical order, but typists frequently went too fast and the keys got jammed. The QWERTY arrangement of keys was designed to slow the typists down. Although there is no longer a problem with jamming, the tradition is still maintained.

Unit C: *Practice Makes Perfect*

## SUMMARY SUMMARY SUMMARY SUMMARY SUMMARY

- You will have learnt to type more accurately with the Touch Typing course, but you will probably need more practice.
- The Typing Tester has helped you to quickly find each of the keyboard keys.
- Plunge and Flying Words tested your typing speed and accuracy.

**TASK** Find a document which you need to produce – a letter, minutes of a meeting or a memo – and practise your typing skills.

# Unit D

## Hardware Basics

### INTRODUCTION

In this unit we will look at the different electronic parts (or *components*) of the computer system, most of which are located in the base unit or tower. The components process and store data.

### Objectives

By the end of this unit you will:

- be familiar with the major components of the computer.
- know the function of each component.
- be familiar with technical terminology associated with hardware.

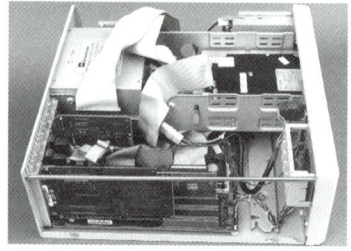

*The inside of a base unit.*

**Key words**

| | |
|---|---|
| Components | The small and large electronic parts of equipment that are inside the base unit and which make computer systems work. |
| Data | Another word for information. *Data* can be words, numbers, sound or pictures – anything that the computer can use. |
| Processor | The component that does things with the data given to it by the keyboard, mouse, etc. |

```
Continue with the computer
```

Unit D: *Hardware Basics*

## THE PROCESSOR

The processor does the computer's 'thinking' (calculating) work. It is made from a small piece of silicon that has microscopic electronic circuits printed on it. This is often called a 'silicon chip' – or just 'chip'. The chip is usually held in a black cover which is plugged into the main circuit board of the computer. Often computers are identified by the type of processor they use, such as the Pentium III processor. Earlier computers used processors identified by numbers, such as the 386 and 486.

### The program and the data

Before the processor can go to work it needs two things:

1. A program to tell it what to do.
2. Data to work with.

When *KeyBytes* did the multiplication tables, the processor used instructions (*the program*) stored in your computer's memory, and also the numbers (*the data*) you typed in on the keyboard.

### Processor speed

The processor speed is measured in **MHz** (megahertz). A clock inside the processor sends out a pulse millions of times each second. Each pulse lets the computer process another piece of data. So a high MHz number shows that the processor will work very fast.

The graph shows how processing speed has increased.

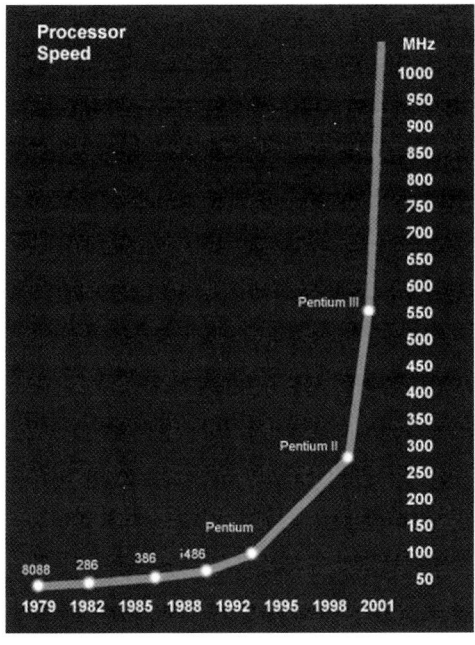

21

Unit D: Hardware Basics

### Other uses of processors

Desktop computers are not the only things to use processors. Processors are also made for a myriad of other equipment, such as microwave ovens, calculators, CD players and video recorders.

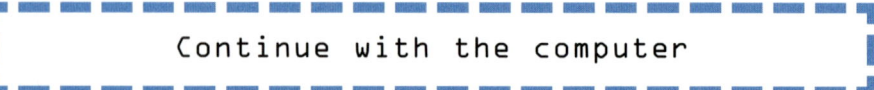

Continue with the computer

## THE COMPUTER'S MEMORY

Computers store instructions and data in their 'memory'. There are different types of memory.

### Permanent memory

When a computer is first switched on it uses instructions that are stored in a *Read Only Memory* (or *ROM*). The computer can 'read' the information but cannot over-write it. The instructions stored in the computer's permanent memory are not changed during normal use by the computer user. And because the memory is 'permanent' the instructions are not lost when the computer is switched off.

### Working memory

However the computer also needs to add to, and take from, a store of instructions and data in a memory it uses while it is working. This data is stored in another type of memory which is usually called *Working Memory*, or *Random Access Memory* or *RAM*.

This memory consists of a number of small silicon chips that look like small versions of the processor chip. These working memory chips can *remember* data, but only while the computer is switched on. This is why it is called working memory. Random Access Memory, temporary memory, internal memory and RAM all mean the same thing.

### Measuring memory: megabytes

The memory is measured in megabytes of RAM. (Bytes and megabytes are explained below.) Some programs need a lot of memory to run efficiently. When buying software programs, it is important to be sure that your computer will have enough memory. You will need to check the minimum requirement for RAM. For example, if your computer has 32 MB (megabytes) of RAM it will easily cope with a program that needs 8 MB of RAM to run. But it will not run a program needing 64 MB.

### Binary code

Each character is stored separately in the memory. The processor converts every character into a code of zeros and ones. One character in this code (for example, 1001010 which is the same as the letter J) takes up *one byte* of memory space.

Roughly 1000 bytes is called a *kilobyte* (KB), just like 1000 grams is called a kilogram. (Actually there are 1024 bytes in a kilobyte, but the approximate number is always used.) If there are approximately 1,000,000 bytes (one million bytes), we refer to this as one *megabyte* (MB). A thousand megabytes is a *gigabyte*.

The code of zeros and ones is called *binary code*. As information is sent in a series of ones and zeros (or digits), this type of information is often called *digital* and other equipment that uses the same code is also referred to as digital: such as digital mobile phones and digital cameras.

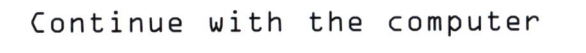

```
Continue with the computer
```

## DATA STORAGE

When the computer is switched off, everything in the computer's working memory (RAM) is lost. So another type of data store is needed. There are several different kinds of data storage devices. A few of the more familiar ones are: *floppy disk*, *hard disk*, *CD-ROM* and *DVD* (digital versatile disk). These devices are usually built into the computer's base unit. Other storage devices include Optical, Zip and Jazz disks.

### Floppy disk

One of the cheapest memory stores is the floppy disk. The outside is made of strong plastic. There is a thin *magnetised* disk inside the plastic case. Data can be read from the disk by putting the floppy disk into the *floppy disk drive*.

Every disk has an opening covered by a metal slide. The disk drive slides this cover to one side, and the computer *reads* data from, or *writes* data to, the magnetised disk. The opening is called the *read window* (see photo, overleaf). If you touch the disk inside the read window there is a chance that your disk will become unusable.

23

Unit D: *Hardware Basics*

There are different kinds of floppy disks but today most computers use 1.44 MB high density (HD) disks. Floppy disks are a simple and cheap way to keep your data safe (letters, lesson plans, notes on themes and projects, etc). Data stored on a floppy disk can be copied into another computer system – and if it is no longer required, the data on the floppy disk can be deleted. Then the disk can be re-used.

*A floppy disk. The cover has been slid to one side to reveal the **read window**.*

If you want to stop some precious data being deleted, you can 'write-protect' the disk. This means that the data cannot be deleted or altered. To do this, slide the little plastic tab so that the square hole in the bottom left corner is covered.

Floppy disks should be kept away from heat, dust and magnets.

```
Continue with the computer
```

### THE HARD DISK

Nearly all computers have a *hard disk* in the base unit. Hard disks are magnetic disks which spin very fast in a dust free box. You can read data from, and write data to, a hard disk.

The hard disk is used to store programs and important data. It works very much faster than a floppy disk. It can store huge amounts of data. Hard disks of 10 gigabytes and more are common. Some computers use more than one hard disk or organise data onto sections (partitions) of a hard disk, so that it seems that there are several disks.

Unit D: *Hardware Basics*

*The inside of a hard disk*

If the hard disk breaks down, then a huge amount of data will be lost. So you should always have a *back-up copy*. This copy can be used to get you going again. Floppy disks, Zip disks, Jazz disks, Optical disks, DVD Tape Drive systems – these can all be used to back up data and small programs.

If your computer is on a network, it uses the hard disk on the *network server*. This will be a very powerful computer linked to several different machines or workstations. Servers have large hard disks and some will have automatic back-up devices. Unit O provides information about networks and network servers.

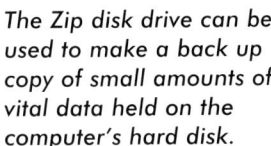

*The Zip disk drive can be used to make a back up copy of small amounts of vital data held on the computer's hard disk.*

### CD-ROM

All sorts of data – including video and sound – can be put onto a CD-ROM.

Two hundred and fifty books, each with 500 pages, will fit onto one CD-ROM. In libraries and at home CD-ROMs are used like reference books.

Unit D: *Hardware Basics*

*All of the volumes of an encyclopaedia will fit on one CD-ROM.*

Programs and games are usually put onto CD-ROMS because CD-ROMS are not easily damaged.

Some CD disk drives only *read* the data from a CD-ROM. Other CD drives *write* new data onto the CD as well.

DVD drives are like CD drives – but they use a different system which puts up to 30 times more data onto DVD. Videos are available on DVD and can be played through the computer. Ordinary CD-ROMs can be read in a DVD drive.

```
Continue with the computer
```

 **OTHER COMPONENTS AND AVOIDING PROBLEMS**

### Power supply

A computer can do nothing without power. The *power supply* converts the power from the wall socket into low voltage current which is needed by the screen, the processor, the memory chips, etc. It also powers a fan to keep the inside of the base unit cool.

Unit D: *Hardware Basics*

### The speaker

A program may also contain sound. This could simply be a bleep to be played when something goes wrong, or it could be an entire piece of music or speech by a famous person. A CD-ROM (or DVD) is often used to run programs containing a lot of sound. Speakers may be built into the computer, otherwise external speakers can also be connected.

### Additional components

You can expand your computer by adding a range of *cards*. A card is a plastic board containing a variety of specialised silicon chips and other electronic components. The card is fitted into a slot inside the computer and usually has an external connection (a *port*) into which the additional component can be plugged. If you are unfamiliar with computers you should seek help when planning to change or add to the components of your computer.

### Sound cards

Most computers now have a sound card. This allows the computer to play stereo sound from CD-ROMs or ordinary music CDs through the computer's speakers with control on features such as the volume, tone, etc.

### Graphics cards

Graphics cards control the appearance of images on the computer (size, colour intensity, speed of change, etc).

### Video capture and TV tuner cards

There are cards available that will allow you to use the computer as a television, or to link it to video-recorders and cameras. Some computers have these built in and most have a space available to add a suitable card.

### Other devices

You can connect many other devices to your computer using special cards or using the range of ports already on the computer. For example, sensors, such as a light meter or a temperature probe, may be connected to computers. Often the required card or connection is included in the purchase of new devices.

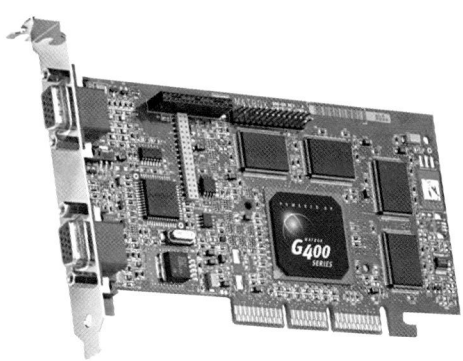

*New components need special cards in the base unit.*

Unit D: *Hardware Basics*

### Computer viruses

A computer's memory can be infected with a *virus*. This can cause many problems, waste time and lose valuable data.

A virus is a program written by someone with malign intent. It can enter your computer without invitation. We use the metaphor of the virus because programs like this can be transferred from one computer to another. A virus can transfer to your computer if an 'infected' floppy disk has been put into the disk drive or infected data has been downloaded from the Internet.

Special *virus protection programs* are available to prevent viruses getting into computers and to remove them. If you have one of these programs in your computer, you should be alerted as soon as a virus appears. Any virus must be removed immediately and if necessary you should get help to do this.

A virus can be very troublesome and dangerous. Some viruses simply produce annoying displays or irritating messages. But there are also really serious viruses, which will delete the contents of an entire hard disk.

To avoid viruses you should follow simple procedures.

1. Use new floppy or other disks that come from a reliable source. Other people's old disks can be a source of problems.

2. Use a virus protection program. Most schools and colleges will have policies about what to use and licences that allow you to use the programs on all the computers.

3. Do not open files, messages or programs that you receive from others without checking them first. Some viruses are sent with e-mail messages and you should be wary of unsolicited items.

> Continue with the computer

# SUMMARY SUMMARY SUMMARY SUMMARY SUMMARY

- Data is processed and stored in the base unit (or tower).
- The processor does the computer's 'calculating' and 'thinking' work.
- Better silicon chip design is enabling processors to work faster and faster.
- The working memory chips are used by the computer to store data while the computer is working.
- Working memory (or random access memory or RAM) only works when the computer is **on**.
- Every character is turned into a code of zeros and ones.
- The name for this code is binary code.
- The code for each character takes up 1 byte of memory space.
- One kilobyte (KB) contains approximately 1000 bytes (1024 to be exact!).
- One megabyte (MB) contains approximately 1000 kilobytes.
- One gigabyte (GB) is approximately 1000 megabytes.
- Floppy disks, hard disks, CD-ROMs and DVDs are all storage devices.
- Data in data storage devices is not lost when the computer's power is switched **off**.
- Most floppy disks store 1.44 MB of data; CD-ROMs store 600 MB of data.
- A hard disk works very much faster than floppy disks and can store much more data.
- You should keep a back-up copy of all the important programs and data that are on your hard disk.
- Programs, pictures and sound are often put onto a CD-ROM or DVD by the manufacturer.
- DVDs can store up to thirty times more data than a CD-ROM.
- Other components can be added to computers by fitting a range of electronic component cards.
- Viruses cause problems and waste time.
- You can protect against viruses by followng simple avoidance procedures and using a virus protection program.

Unit D: *Hardware Basics*

**TASKS**

1. Find out about the computer you use most often.

   What type of processor does it have?
   What is the processor speed?
   What size is the Random Access Memory?
   How large is the hard disk?
   What other data storage devices does it have?

   Ask your colleagues for help with this if necessary.

2. Find out if your school or college has any sensing equipment. Talk to the staff who use the sensing equipment about classroom applications.

# Unit E

# Screen Technology

## INTRODUCTION

Computer systems rely on a range of equipment to help the user carry out a variety of tasks. The screen on which text and images are displayed and the printer which produces copies of the work, are just two of the many devices that may be part of the system you are using. As different technologies develop, the types of equipment available for teachers and the facilities that these provide are constantly expanding.

## Objectives

In this unit we will be looking at the way in which computers display text and images.

By the end of this unit you will:

- be familiar with a range of display equipment.
- have some understanding of the technology that the equipment uses.

**Key words**

| | |
|---|---|
| Input | To put *in* to the computer. A keyboard or other devices are used to input the information. |
| Output | To send *out* from the computer. The computer processes data and then outputs it to the screen or printer. |

---

Continue with the computer

---

Unit E: *Screen Technology*

# SCREEN TECHNOLOGY

A computer uses a screen to display text and images. The screen is usually contained in a separate piece of equipment and this is often called the *monitor* or *VDU* (visual display unit). A few computers, such as some Macintosh machines, include the screen in the base unit, so there is no separate monitor. Laptop and other portable computers also have integrated screens.

A monitor is an *output device*. The computer outputs (or sends) information to it: just as it outputs information to printers or loudspeakers.

There are many different types of screen technology, each used for a different purpose. In this unit we consider some of the technologies available and why each is used.

## The Cathode Ray Tube

The most common monitors use a screen that is based on the cathode ray tube (CRT). CRTs work by firing a pattern of rays from the rear of the monitor onto the screen. The inside of the screen is coated with a material which lights up when the ray hits it. Cathode Ray Tubes were invented in the 1930s and have also been important in equipment such as televisions and radar sets. Cathode ray technology has not changed very much since computers became common, except that colour is now accepted as standard. (Originally computers had monochrome monitors that only displayed one colour [or white] and black.)

The number of colours that can be displayed by the monitor depends on the graphics card used in the computer's base unit. All graphics cards are able to display 16 colours, most will display 256 colours and it is now common for a graphics card to display 16.7 million colours.

*Even stylish CRT monitors are bulky and heavy.*

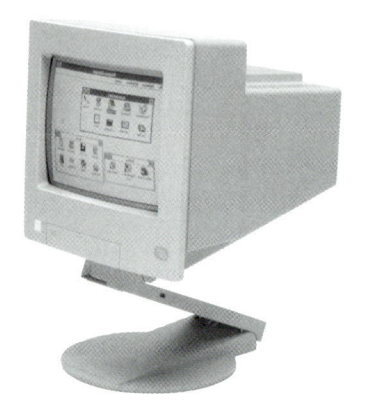

```
Continue with the computer
```

Unit E: *Screen Technology*

## LIQUID-CRYSTAL DISPLAY SCREENS

Portable computers, such as laptops or palmtops, often use Liquid-Crystal Display (LCD) screens. These screens contain a transparent crystal in liquid form. When electricity is passed through the liquid, it appears darker or coloured in the required areas. Other areas remain transparent.

LCD screens are flat and very light. They use very small amounts of power, which means that they can easily run from a battery. The screens can be made to fit inside the lid of a laptop or palmtop. Some lower-cost LCD screens do not provide a very bright image and can be difficult to read in sunlight. On more expensive computers the LCD screen is often lit from behind to improve the brightness.

*LCD screens are very slim and light.*

As LCD technology has improved, larger and brighter screens have become available, making them easier to use. However, LCD screens can still be difficult to read from the side and it is difficult for several people to view the display at the same time.

*Soon LCD screens will replace CRT screens for desktop computers.*

```
Continue with the computer
```

## PIXELS AND RESOLUTION

Everything that is displayed on the screen is made up of small square dots, which are known as *pixels*. Originally the name came from the term **PIC**ture **EL**ement**S**, then the C was changed to X.

The number of pixels used on a screen is referred to as the 'screen resolution'. High-resolution screens use a high number of pixels to display text and images; low-resolution screens use a low number of pixels.

Unit E: *Screen Technology*

High resolution allows very fine lines and details to be displayed more accurately. Often high-resolution screens and their associated graphics cards are capable of displaying a high number of colours. Generally, the higher the resolution, the greater the cost of equipment.

A program (such as *KeyBytes*) may use a display of 600 by 800 pixels. This is called SVGA resolution and allows a program to run on inexpensive equipment. Programs designed to be run on low-resolution equipment will run on a high-resolution machine.

Sometimes running a program on a screen with low resolution gives the text or other images an odd appearance as the individual pixels are enlarged and there is insufficient space on the screen to display the entire screen. Large screens have the advantage of high levels of resolution: so video projectors benefit from being connected to computers capable of high-resolution output.

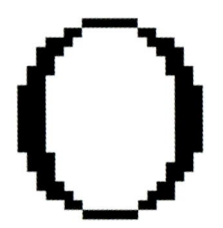

*The letter 'O' has been enlarged by 800% to show the pixels and their effect.*

Continue with the computer

## TOUCH SCREENS, SCREEN SAVERS AND POWER MANAGEMENT

### Touch screens

Touch screens are often found where information is provided to the public, for example in museums and tourist information offices. Touch screens are also often used where a limited amount of information is related directly to a calculation; for example on cash registers in fast food outlets. No mouse or keyboard are needed when using a touch screen: all that's necessary is to simply touch the option required.

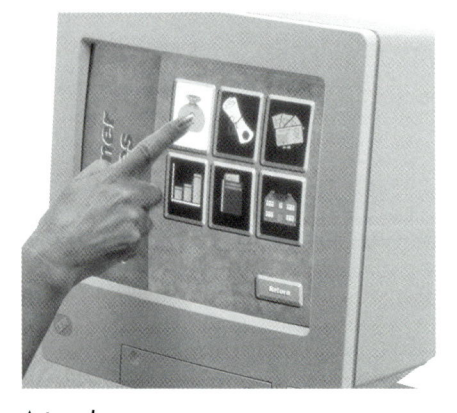

*A touch screen*

Ordinary screens cannot be turned into a touch screen. The earliest touch screens had fine wires within the glass screen, sensitive to the touch of a finger but touch screen technology is developing rapidly.

Now touch screens are available for handheld palmtop computers. The screens respond to a pen or stylus. These touch-screen computers can be used to recognise handwriting and they also allow direct input of complex information.

### Screen savers

If the same picture is displayed on a screen for many hours, the picture can 'burn' into the screen. The burnt-in picture becomes a 'ghost' on the screen. To prevent this, you can use a screen saver. This is a small program that runs automatically when the keyboard and mouse have not been used for some time. The program displays a continually moving picture so that the display cannot become burnt-in. There are thousands of screen saver programs available and computers are usually supplied with some already installed. Some screen saver programs allow you to display your own moving messages. The display is returned to normal as soon as the mouse is moved or keyboard touched.

### Saving power

While the monitor remains switched on it uses electricity, even if only the screen saver is running. This is true for other components, such as hard-disk drives. Most computers are able to switch off the power to a component automatically after a set time using a power-management program. The power-management program will switch the screen or other components back on as soon as the mouse is moved again or a keyboard key is used.

---

Continue with the computer

---

## OTHER TYPES OF DISPLAY

Information from the computer may also be projected onto a screen. In common with other projection systems, the screen is a white surface that will provide a bright image. However, the projector is more than just a powerful light source since it also translates data into a form suitable for display and projection and uses LCD technology to project that display. The projectors used to do this will often project video images as well as text and pictures and are commonly called LCD or video projectors.

The information from a computer may also be projected using a special transparent screen placed on an overhead projector (OHP). This type of screen is sometimes called a *tablet*. Although they are generally cheaper than projectors, tablets require powerful OHPs in order to be effective.

**Interactive whiteboards**

Using computers with groups of people usually requires a very large monitor or a screen and a projector. Whiteboards are now available that use touch screen technology to allow the board to act as both a screen, to show the display from the computer, and as an input device to control the computer. For example a teacher may display drawings, pictures or video clips to a class and then use a pointer (or even a finger) as a mouse to open a program or file from the computer.

Interactive whiteboards allow teachers to operate a computer 'remotely': there is no need for the teacher to be at the usual monitor and keyboard.

*This shows a teacher writing on an electronic whiteboard with an electronic pen.*

**Video conferencing**

Meetings can cost a great deal if people need to travel to be with each other. A cheaper solution is to use video conferencing. This allows all the participants to talk with, and see on their screens, all the others involved in the discussion. To set up a video conference, a video camera, a computer and microphone must be placed in front of each person or group of people, who are to take part.

*Video conferencing at Bradford CTC.*

Live pictures and sound from each position are sent to all the other participants using the telecommunications networks. This can be around the world if necessary.

In some places video conferencing is used by schools to allow teachers to work with students in remote areas. This allows children to remain in their home village or town, and gives small schools access to specialist subject teachers. Applications of video conferencing being developed in schools include uses in modern foreign languages and to provide 'experts in the classroom': i.e. activities associated with museums and industry etc.

Video conferencing is available relatively cheaply to home users of computers, and home computers can easily have small video cameras attached to them.

### Virtual reality

*Virtual reality takes you into the computer's world.*

Virtual reality gives the illusion of entering a world created by a computer program. Three-dimensional images are displayed on screens in a special headset, and devices such as gloves with sensors, are used in place of the keyboard or mouse.

For example, architects are now able to provide clients with a three-dimensional impression of a building design. Applications such as this are also becoming increasingly important in engineering.

### Simulators

Simulators are machines that use screens to display images that seem to place the user in a real situation. These have been used for some time in driving schools and for the training of aircraft pilots. Theme parks use complex computer programs in simulators to give visitors the illusion of being in different worlds. There are simulators for many different sporting activities, from golf to skiing.

*Airline pilots train on simulators.*

Unit E: *Screen Technology*

> Continue with the computer

## SUMMARY   SUMMARY   SUMMARY   SUMMARY   SUMMARY

- A screen outputs data processed by the computer.
- Most full size monitors currently use Cathode Ray Tubes (CRTs).
- Colour monitors display at least 16 colours; many display up to 16.7 million colours.
- The computer's graphics card determines the number of colours to be sent to the monitor.
- Laptop computers use a Liquid-Crystal Display (LCD) screen.
- LCD screens are flatter, lighter and use less power than CRT screens.
- All images on screens are made up from pixels, which are small square dots of colour.
- High-resolution screens use more pixels.
- Very fine details can be shown more accurately on a high-resolution screen.
- With a touch screen, a mouse or keyboard is unnecessary: a finger, pen or stylus is used instead.
- Touch screens are often used where the public needs to find information or the information required to be input is very limited.
- Screen savers prevent screen burn where a 'ghost' of an image is left on the screen.
- Some monitors switch off automatically, using a power-saving program.
- Interactive whiteboards are huge screens displaying output from the computer and allowing input by finger or electronic pen.
- Video conferencing allows visual communication across distances.
- Virtual reality gives the illusion of entering a 'real' situation. It can seem like you are actually inside a building or inspecting an engineering project that is complete.

**TASKS**

1. What types of display are available in your school? Do you have access to large monitors or interactive whiteboards?

2. How would you use an LCD projector, a large monitor or interactive whiteboard in your own subject?

3. If you are interested in learning more about equipment mentioned here, you will find that many companies selling this equipment will provide demonstrations through the Web.

# Unit F

# Peripherals

## INTRODUCTION

By now you are quite familiar with the main computer system hardware and the screen technology that displays the text and images. This unit is about the extra equipment that you can connect to your computer, such as printers, cameras, scanners, joysticks and modems.

This equipment is called *peripheral* equipment. You can easily connect and disconnect most peripheral equipment from the computer without stopping the computer from working normally. Some peripherals are used to give information (data) to the computer. These are 'input devices'. Others are used to get data out of the computer. They are called 'output devices'.

All peripherals connect up to the computer.

### Objectives

In this unit you will:

- learn about different peripheral devices.
- consider appropriate uses of different devices.

**Key words**

| | |
|---|---|
| Binary code | The code of zeros and ones used by computers. |
| Convert | In the computing sense, it means to turn text or images into binary code. |
| Device | A single piece of equipment that is usually designed to perform only one function. |
| Digital | A device that uses binary code as its 'language', such as digital television, digital camera, etc. |
| Download | To move digital data into a computer from an external source. For example, to download images from a digital camera or the Internet. |
| Internet | A worldwide network of data. |

> Continue with the computer

## OUTPUT DEVICES – PRINTERS

Like screens, printers are output devices. The data from the computer is sent to the printer and 'displayed' as printed text and images. There are different types of printer available.

### Dot-matrix printers

Dot-matrix printers are now quite old-fashioned. They have a print head that goes backwards and forwards across the paper. The print head contains 9 or 24 steel pins that hit the paper through an inked ribbon. These make small dots on the paper. Together, the group of small dots forms a letter or drawing.

Dot-matrix printers are noisy, but inexpensive to buy and cheap to run.

For home and school use, dot-matrix printers are becoming rare. Other types of printer give much better print quality and are much faster. Many businesses prefer the higher quality images of other printers. However, a dot-matrix printer can print easily on *multi-layer forms* because the pressure of the steel pins transfers the image through the thickness of paper. For this reason small dot-matrix printers are still in use in most shops or ticket agencies.

*A shop receipt printed using a dot-matrix printer.*

### Laser printers

Like the dot-matrix printer, laser printers print using dots, but in greater quantity. Most laser printers print at least 240 dots per centimetre. This is usually referred to as 600 dots per inch (dpi) because Americans use inches. They are so close together that you cannot see the individual dots. The line looks as if it has been drawn by a pen.

Laser printers work by shining a very thin pattern of laser light onto a metal drum. *Toner* (a black powder) sticks to the parts of the drum that have been 'exposed' by the laser light. The drum then prints the toner

Unit F: *Peripherals*

onto the page. Before the page is pushed out of the printer, it is rolled and heated to bind the toner to the page. This is why pages from a laser printer are always warm.

Laser printers are fast and quiet, and give very good print quality. As the technology improves, higher resolutions are becoming possible. The quality of output of the latest colour laser printers is very high.

P

*A laser printed character*

*A laser printer*

### Inkjet printers

Inkjet printers also make the text and pictures out of dots. They work by squirting fine droplets of ink onto paper. The droplets are about one millionth of the size of a drop of water from an eyedropper. The print quality can be very good – often as good as some laser printers – and the equipment is usually cheaper. Like laser printers, inkjet printers also work quietly and can be quite fast.

Inkjet printers are the most popular choice for colour printing. They use four ink colours: magenta, cyan, yellow and black. These coloured inks are combined on the page to make all the different colours. The inks are in cartridges, which can be replaced when empty.

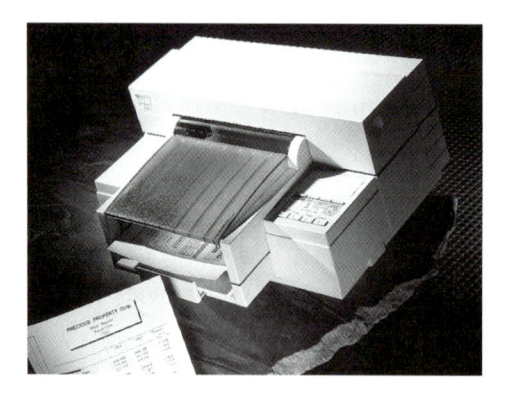

*An inkjet printer*

*Each of the four coloured ink cartridges can be replaced when empty.*

Continue with the computer

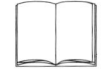

## MORE OUTPUT DEVICES

Ordinary computer printers are not always suitable for all uses. Specialised drawings, such as architect's plans and engineering designs, require a different type of printer, such as a plotter.

### Plotters

One of the simplest types of plotter works by moving a pen across a flat page. Others hold the paper over a drum and move the drum and pen to produce the plot. Sometimes, only one pen is used, but it is more common for the penholder to contain several different pens for different colours.

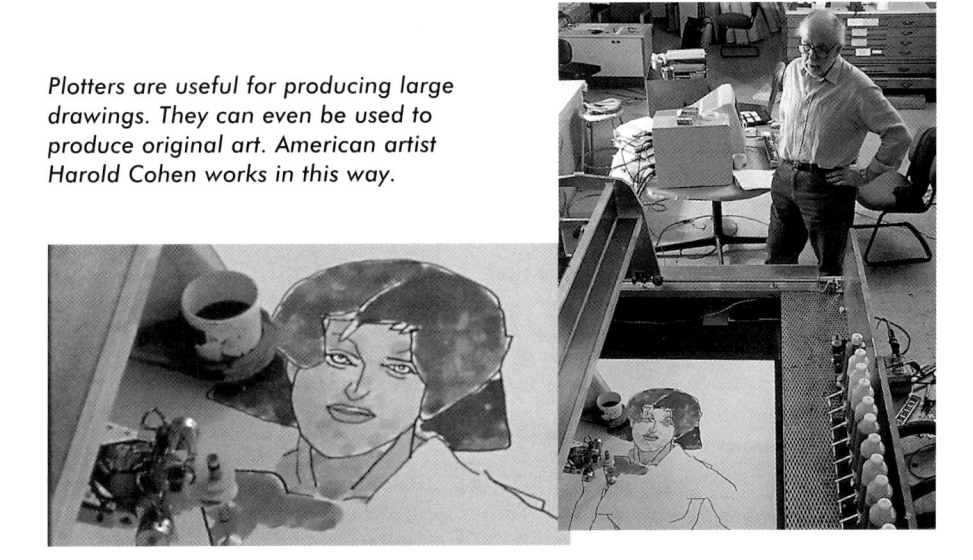

*Plotters are useful for producing large drawings. They can even be used to produce original art. American artist Harold Cohen works in this way.*

### Printing posters

Large inkjet printers can be used to print colour posters. They are slow but print to a very high quality on all types of paper and plastic.

*A poster being printed by inkjet printer.*

Very large laser printers can also be used for large documents, but they are very expensive.

Unit F: *Peripherals*

> Continue with the computer

## DIGITAL INPUT DEVICES

Scanners, digital cameras and joysticks are all input devices. In other words, they can be used to enter data into your computer. Some devices are used for both input and output.

### Scanners

Images, such as drawings or photos, can be input to a computer using a *scanner*. The scanner *reads* the image, converting the information to a digital form and displays it on the computer screen. The image can then be combined with other documents – and at any time can be printed. Most of the images that you see in *KeyBytes* were input into a computer using a scanner.

*Hand-held scanners can be used to input small images.*

Scanners that are dragged across an image by hand are called *hand-held* scanners. They are about twice the size of a mouse. The size of image that can be scanned by a hand-held scanner is very limited.

A more popular scanner is a *flatbed* scanner. This can scan larger pieces of paper. Other types of scanners are built into photocopiers or printers. Some computer retailers now offer scanners with computer systems as part of the standard computer system.

*A flatbed scanner*

As the size of the area to be scanned increases, so the scanner becomes more expensive. However, this is another area where the development of technology has reduced the price of equipment, and A4 and even A3 scanners are common. Some scanners are specifically designed to scan photographic transparencies and film negatives.

Scanners can also be used to input printed text documents. Provided that the printed text is reasonably clear, special software can *read* each character. If there are spelling mistakes, these can be corrected automatically. It is possible to then modify or add to the text. The process using such software to read printed text is called *optical character recognition* (OCR).

## Digital cameras

Digital cameras and digital video cameras may also be used with computers. Unlike conventional cameras that use film, digital cameras record images in digital formats as binary code. This means that their images can be transferred directly into a computer. The quality of the image depends on the optical quality of the lens and the screen resolution of which the camera is capable. Some cameras allow a choice of high or low resolutions.

Digital cameras use LCD screens as viewfinders and the range of facilities that the camera offers may be shown as a menu on the screen. The images may be stored in the camera and then downloaded into the computer via a cable. Other systems use a removable card, so that the user is not limited to the storage capacity of the camera. There are also cameras that store the images on an ordinary floppy disk or on a smaller sized re-usable disk. The disk can be taken from the camera and used in the computer immediately, without having to download the images through a cable.

Digital video cameras commonly use types of tape cartridge, but still record in digital format. A cable connection to a video capture card or serial port in the computer allows you to watch the video. Digital video systems are also compatible with video recorders for use with televisions.

Both still and video cameras use batteries and some use a lot of power. Rechargeable batteries supplied by the manufacturers have made this power use relatively inexpensive. Unit N provides ideas for classroom applications.

*Photos from digital cameras don't need scanning.*

## Joysticks

Many people use the computer to play games. A useful peripheral device when playing games is the *joystick*. It is a moveable handle with one or more firing buttons on the handle. If, for example, you are playing a 'shoot 'em up' space game, you use the handle to move your spacecraft and then fire at alien ships using the firing button. Varieties of joystick may include steering wheels or foot pedals to give a more realistic feel to the game. Some now have some feedback devices to give the player a sense of response from the program.

Joysticks are also used for more serious purposes to control heavy machinery, or in dangerous situations. Large cranes and digging equipment can be controlled remotely, for example.

*A joystick*

Unit F: *Peripherals*

## MODEM – an input and output device

A modem is used to connect a computer to a telephone line. Once connected it is possible to send or collect data from any other computer in the world, provided that the other computer is also connected to a modem and a telephone line.

Modems may be built into a computer in the form of a modem card, or be external in a small box, attached by cable to your computer. Portable computers may have modems built in or small cards that are inserted into special slots in a laptop.

Before the modem connects to the other computer your computer must be told which phone number to call. Your computer's modem then calls this number, waits for the other modem to answer, then transfers data. The data transfers using binary code.

*Wireless modems* can be used to send data using a radio transmitter: and mobile phone networks can also transfer data. Some mobile phones have e-mail facilities and others allow you to plug your computer's modem into the phone itself.

A modem must be used to send e-mail messages or to connect to the Internet. You will find out more about this later.

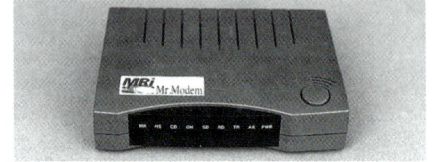

*A modem connects each computer to a telephone line.*

```
Continue with the computer
```

## HARDWARE AND SOFTWARE

The terms *hardware* and *software* were mentioned earlier. Hardware refers to the parts of a computer that you can see and touch, such as the monitor, keyboard and mouse. The term hardware is also used to cover all the electronic parts inside the base unit. Software refers to the programs the computer needs to work. Examples of software include games programs, word-processor programs and drawing programs. A computer cannot work without software.

*A CD-ROM holding software that took hundreds of thousands of hours to develop.*

Most software takes at least hundreds of hours to prepare ready for others to use. Some takes hundreds of thousands of hours, with teams of specialists working on different parts of complex programs. This is very costly and the work is protected by copyright laws. If a program is copied for someone else to use without permission, that is theft, and some companies work very hard to trace pirated software.

Pirated software may also include viruses or errors (called *bugs*) that can affect a whole computer system.

### Driver programs

Every peripheral needs a special piece of software to make it work. This is called a 'driver program' – or 'hardware driver'. These small programs give all the instructions the computer needs to work with the peripheral and must be loaded onto the computer's hard disk before the peripheral can carry out its function. A common example of the need for a particular driver is that if you change your printer you will need to select the printer driver written for this printer.

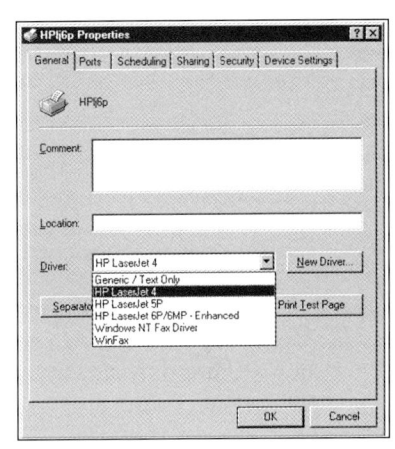

*All peripherals need a 'driver program'.*

### Peripherals for special purposes

Peripherals are available for many different uses. Here are short notes on a few:

**Graphics tablets** – used by designers. It lets them 'draw' their designs with an 'electronic pen' or 'brush'.

**Speakers** – your computer might have two of these already. For higher quality sound, extra speakers and a control box are sometimes used.

*High specification PC with extra speakers and control box.*

**Microphone** – when a microphone and voice-recognition software are added to a computer the programs associated with the voice-recognition software can be made to act on your spoken instructions.

## Unit F: Peripherals

**Music keyboards** – music, played on the keyboard, can be stored on the computer's hard disk. The computer can even produce the music score.

*A music keyboard that inputs to, and outputs from, computer systems.*

**Data loggers** – main uses include:

- Measuring how often something happens, for example, how many cars travel along a road each hour of each day.
- Measuring things that change, for example, how much water is in an area of soil throughout the year.

Using information collected by a datalogger and a modelling program on a computer:

- Road planners can judge whether the road needs widening or a bypass is necessary.
- A winegrower can find out why vines in some parts of the vineyard do not grow as well as in other parts.

*A data logger to measure soil moisture.*

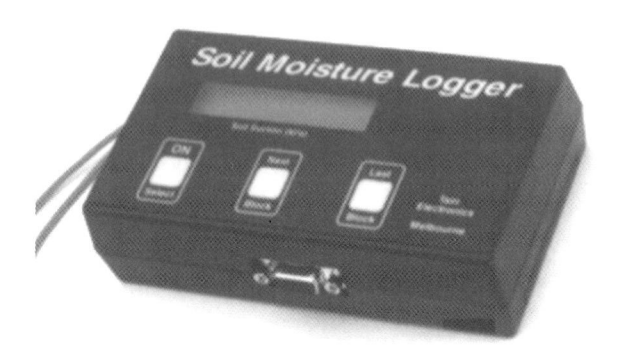

Data logging devices are particularly useful in science, geography and maths. There are a number of devices for data logging made specifically for use in schools.

Unit F: *Peripherals*

## SUMMARY   SUMMARY   SUMMARY   SUMMARY   SUMMARY

- Input devices give information (data) to the computer.
- Ouput devices are used to get data out of the computer.
- Peripherals are all the extra pieces of hardware that connect to the computer.
- Dot-matrix printers are cheap but noisy. They are mainly used where quality is not important or where multi-layer forms must be printed. They print using a series of ink dots.
- Laser printers give prints of very high quality because they use more than 240 dots of black toner on each centimetre of print.
- An inkjet printer is very good for low-cost colour printing and gives good quality black printing.
- Colour prints can be produced on inkjet printers and laser printers.
- Plotters are used to produce very large drawings and large inkjet printers are often used to print posters in colour.
- Pictures and text can be input into a computer using a scanner.
- Photos taken with a digital camera do not need scanning as the images are already in binary code.
- Digital equipment works by using binary code as its 'language'.
- Joysticks are not just useful for games: they are also used for heavy and dangerous work.
- A modem is used to connect a computer to a phone system.
- Hardware is the word used for the parts of a computer you can see and touch.
- Software is the word used for the computer's programs.
- Each peripheral needs special software to be on the computer's hard disk to make the peripheral work. Each piece of special software is called a 'driver program'.
- Software copyright belongs to the person who designed it. Copying software for someone else infringes copyright laws.
- There are many peripherals that perform a variety of functions: graphics tablets, speakers, microphones, music keyboards and data loggers are just a few examples.

Unit F: *Peripherals*

**TASKS**

1. Find out what peripherals are available in your school. Discuss their value for educational purposes with teachers who use them.

2. Consider the ways in which data loggers, a scanner or digital camera could be used for a specific topic. Find out what is available in your school or perhaps what you could borrow from another institution. Select a unit of work and decide how the use of these devices would enhance the learning of your students. Test your ideas.

# Unit G
# Working with Windows

## INTRODUCTION

This unit focuses on the *Windows* program. Windows is the 'operating system' used by your computer to operate and control the computer's electronic systems.

The Windows operating system starts up and assumes control of your computer's functions each time you start your computer.

## Objectives

In this unit you will:

- gain a better understanding of the Windows operating system.
- learn how to start a program, open and create folders.
- learn about icons, menus and dialogue boxes.
- learn how to get help from the computer.

**Key words**

**Context sensitive** — This is 'computer jargon' which means 'depending on what is happening at the time'. For example: if you are about to print a page and you click on Help, the program guesses that you want to know about printing a page. So 'context sensitive help' should give you information on 'printing'.

**Graphical** — Use of drawings, pictures, photographs to give information or tell a story.

**Interface** — Computers work with electronic data, whereas people work with text and pictures. Where the two operations interact is called an interface.

---

> Continue with the computer

Unit G: *Working with Windows*

## WHAT IS WINDOWS?

Windows is 'user friendly' compared with earlier operating systems. You do not need to remember complicated instructions. Windows uses pictures (icons) to guide you. Pointing and clicking with the mouse on these icons gives instructions to the program.

There are several 'windows operating systems'. The best known were created by Microsoft: Windows 3.11, Windows 95, Windows 98, Windows 2000, etc. Unless you use a Macintosh, it is likely that your computer uses one of these. All types of 'windows operating systems' work with icons and the mouse. This type of program is often called a GUI (short for 'graphical user interface').

```
Continue with the computer
```

## STARTING A PROGRAM AND OPENING FOLDERS

The Start screen for Windows is often called the 'Desktop'. Usually, icons for the most often used programs and folders are kept on the Desktop. If you want to open one of these folders, or start one of the programs, just double-click on its icon.

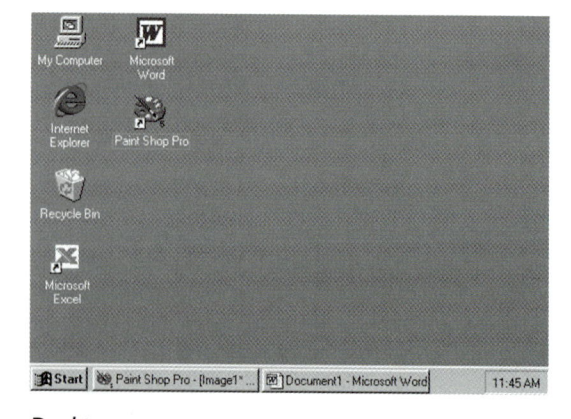

*Desktop screen*

Unit G: Working with Windows

Inside these folders you will find other folders and programs. If you double-click on a program, it starts up, ready for you to use.

More than one program can be working at a time. This is often very useful – you will find out why later in *KeyBytes*. When you look on the Taskbar, you will see what programs are running, or what files are still open.

*The Taskbar: notice the Start button in the left hand corner. You can see that Microsoft Word and Paint Shop Pro programs are both running.*

More folders can be opened, and programs can be started, from the Start button. When you click the Start button, a Start menu pops up. Choices made on this Start menu take you on to other menus and other choices. One of the Start menu choices is to Shut Down Windows. You should always do this before switching off the computer.

*This Start menu pops up when you click on the Start button*

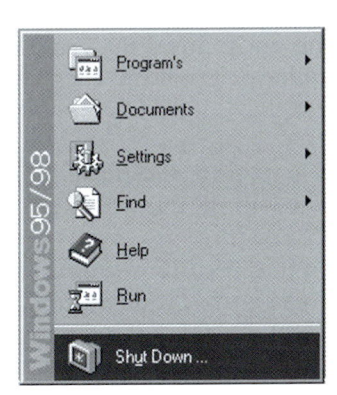

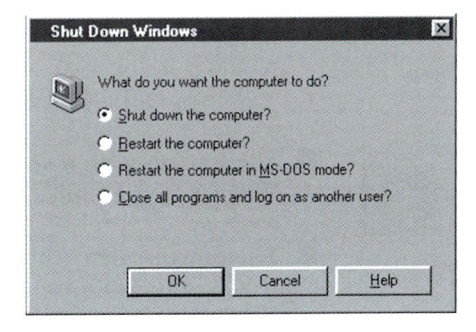

*Shut Down dialogue screen*

```
Continue with the computer
```

## A CLOSER LOOK AT WINDOWS

- Along the top is the ***Title bar*** (number 1 on the picture over the page). This gives the name of the open window. The name will be the folder's name; or the program name; or the program name and the name of the open file.

53

Unit G: *Working with Windows*

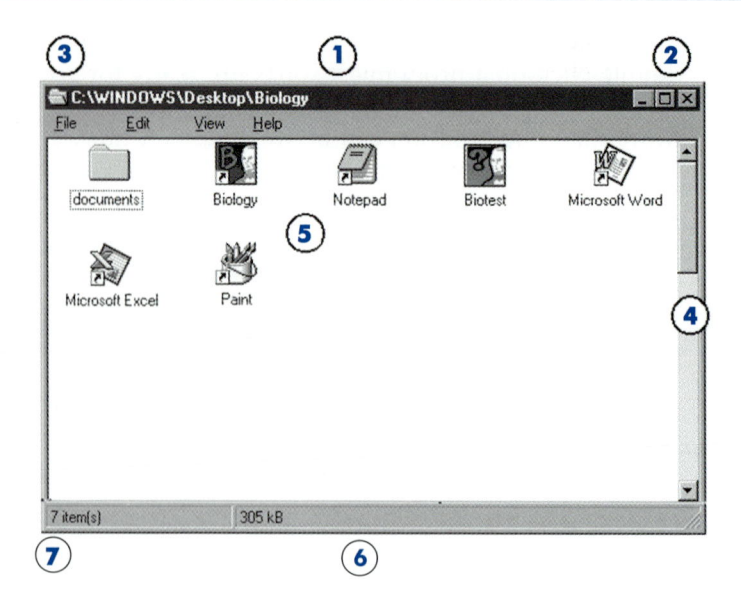

- At the top, on the right, are three buttons (number 2 on the picture).

**Close**

- The button with an **X** is used to close the window. If the window is a 'program window', then clicking on **X** closes the program. If the window is for a file within a folder or program, then clicking on it will close only the file.

**Maximise**

- The button with a square on it is used to *maximise* the window. When you maximise a window it will fill the whole screen.

**Minimise**

- The button with a little dash on it is used to *minimise* the window. When you minimise a window you shrink it down to a button on the Taskbar (number 6 on the picture). You can see the minimised buttons for Microsoft Word and Paint Shop Pro on the previous page. These show the programs are still running, but their windows are minimised.

**Restore**

- Sometimes the maximise button turns into two small squares. This happens when you have changed the window's size. Click on the two small squares and the window goes back to its old size. It *restores* the window to its old size.

- At the top, on the left, there is a small icon (number 3 on the picture). The icon looks different in every program but it works in the same way. Clicking on this icon opens the *System menu*. The System menu can also be used to Close, Maximise, Minimise or Restore the window.

*System menu*

54

Unit G: Working with Windows

- The contents of a window are sometimes greater than you can see on one screen. The window will then have *scrollbars* (number 4 on the picture). You can use these to look at the whole of the contents. Do this by dragging the small square *scrollbar block*, or by clicking on the *scrollbar arrows*.

Internet Explorer
*A program icon*

- Programs and folders you use most often usually have their own icon on the start screen (number 5 on the picture). There are two kinds of icon: a program icon and a folder icon.

- When you double-click on a program icon, it starts the program.

My Documents
*A folder icon*

- When you double-click on a folder icon, it opens a window. In the window you will find other icons. These will be for programs, or for more folders, or for more of both.

- Just to remind you, along the bottom of every screen is the *Taskbar* (number 6 on the picture). The Taskbar buttons show which programs are still running, and which folders are still open.

- At the beginning of the Taskbar is the Start button (number 7 on the picture). Click on the Start button, and then on its Start menu to find many other menu choices.

```
Continue with the computer
```

## MENU CHOICES

Most windows have a *Menu bar* just under the Title bar. Click any word on the Menu bar and a menu choice drops down. Each choice on the menu is an instruction for the computer. If you want to make a choice from the menu, just click on the instruction. If you decide you **do not** want to do anything, then just click *to one side of* the menu.

*Menu choices such as this drop down when you click on any word in the Menu bar.*

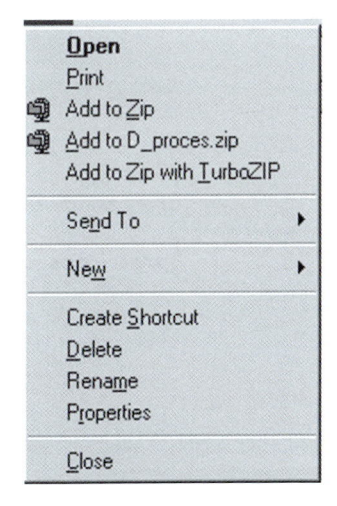

| |
|---|
| **Open** |
| Print |
| Add to Zip |
| Add to D_proces.zip |
| Add to Zip with TurboZIP |
| Send To ▶ |
| New ▶ |
| Create Shortcut |
| Delete |
| Rename |
| Properties |
| Close |

## Main menus

These are usually lists of options like the Edit menu shown in the picture. The simple way to select an option is to just click on your choice.

If you often make that same choice, then it is worth learning the 'Shortcut'. You can work faster – if you are typing there is no need to stop to move the mouse. You can find out which are the Shortcut keys from each of the menus. Look at 'Copy' in the picture. The Shortcut key for Copy is Ctrl+C. (This means press the Ctrl key and the C key together.)

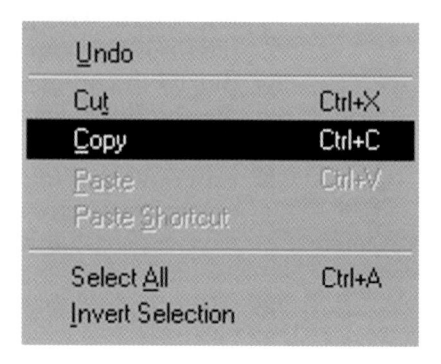

*This menu drops down when you click on Edit in the Menu bar.*

## Off or On choices

Items on the menu can be switched *on* or *off*. If an option has a tick, or a bullet, or a cross in front of it, then it is switched on. If it has not, then it is switched off. Clicking the option turns it from off to on (or on to off). Here are a few examples:

*This tick turns the Windows toolbars*

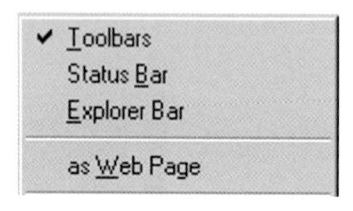

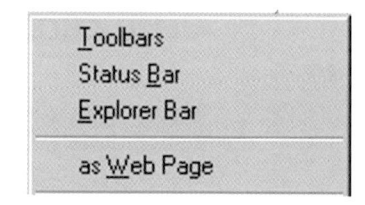

**on ...**                                    **... and off**

*The position of the blob changes the view from*

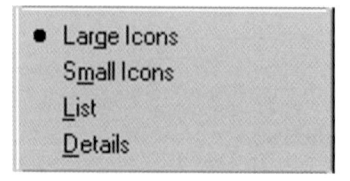

**large icons ...**                           **... to small icons**

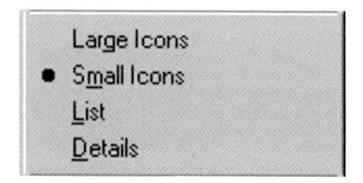

Unit G: *Working with Windows*

### Click left or click right?

Most of the time you must use the *left* mouse button. Use the left button to start programs, open folders, make choices, etc. Sometimes, you will need to use the *right* mouse button. This will show you some different menus.

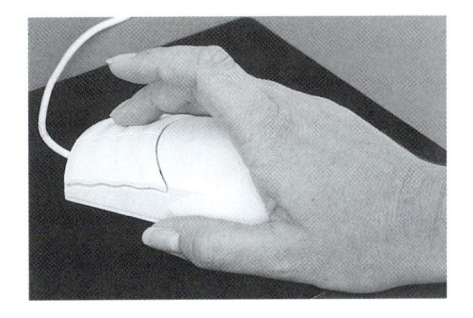

> Continue with the computer

## DIALOGUE BOXES

Windows sometimes needs information from you in order to perform a task: for example a password may be required before the program can proceed.

*Some dialogue screens need an answer. This one needs a password to be typed.*

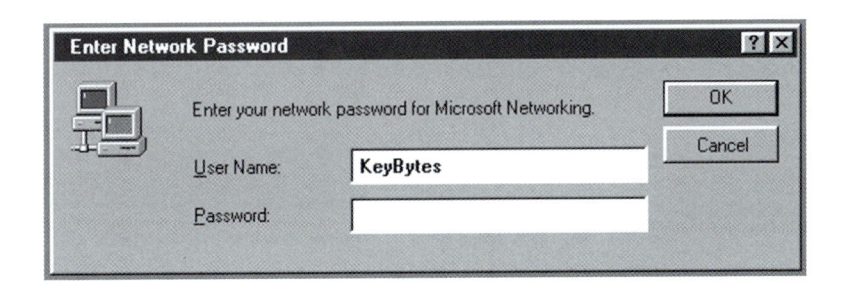

In the example shown, the dialogue box is quite simple: when you have typed the correct password, you click on the 'OK' button, and the computer carries out your instructions.

Some dialogue windows remind you that you need to click on a certain button or make sure that there is a disk in the disk drive; others ask you to verify that you want to proceed with a course of action.

If you open a dialogue window, but decide you don't want to answer it, then just click the 'Cancel' button.

*This dialogue screen asks if you want to save a file before the program closes.*

57

Unit G: *Working with Windows*

### Lists and tabs

The dialogue window quite often has too many options to list in an ordinary menu. If this happens there is usually a list you can scroll through before selecting an option. Sometimes you need to click on an arrow, then a list of options drops down. Some dialogue windows have more than one 'page'.

The dialogue window shown here has three pages. To see one of the two other pages click on one of the tabs at the top: 'Name & Location' or 'Advanced'.

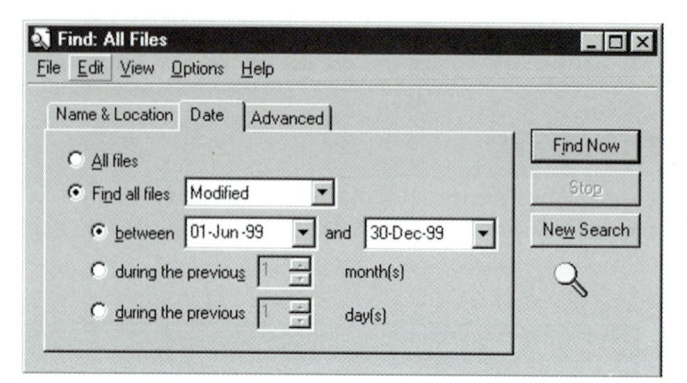

*Here is a dialogue window which can be answered in various ways.*

```
Continue with the computer
```

### GETTING HELP

If you cannot work out how to do something, the program might be able to give you help. This help can be accessed by clicking on 'Help' on the program's Menu bar.

There is sometimes a choice of two or three types of Help. Some types of Help let you type in a question. You are then given the help screen that matches your query. Others ask questions. After you have clicked on the answers, the program gives you the help screen it thinks you need.

With both types of Help system, you will probably have to go through more than one help screen and make other choices to find what you want. With persistence, you should finally pinpoint the help that you need. With practice, you will become faster and more proficient at getting help.

Unit G: *Working with Windows*

*The Help menu drops down when you click on 'Help' in the Menu bar.*

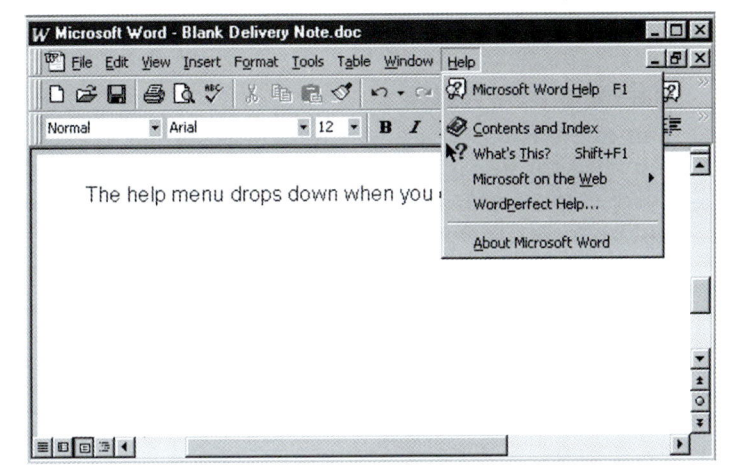

You may find it useful to print the help screen so that you can follow the instructions more easily. You can do this by using its menu bar.

*Print the help screen by using its own Menu bar.*

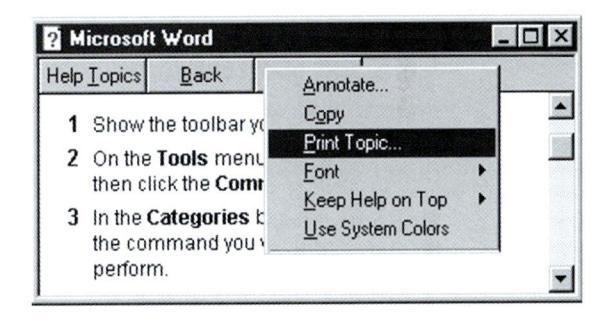

## Context sensitive help

Context sensitive help is available with some programs. This is easier to use but usually it does not cover everything you might want to know. With context sensitive help just hold the pointer over the item that you want to know about – and click.

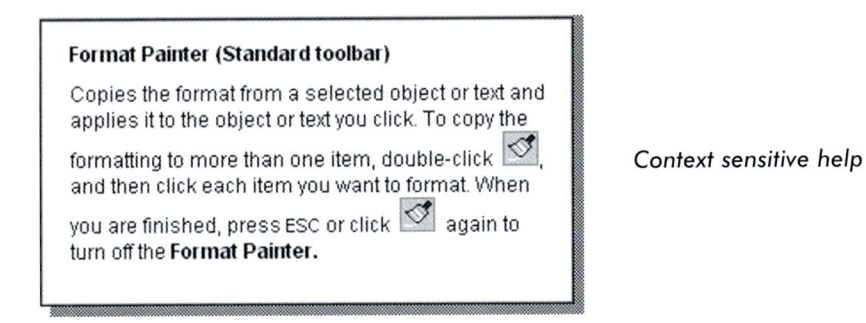

*Context sensitive help*

```
Continue with the computer
```

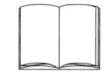

## FOLDERS, ICONS AND SHORTCUTS

### Making a new folder

You can make as many new folders as you need for new files or programs. There is more than one way to do this and each way is slightly different. Whichever way you decide to do it, you always have to choose: 'New' and 'Folder' on a menu. One of these menus appears if you right-click anywhere on the desktop.

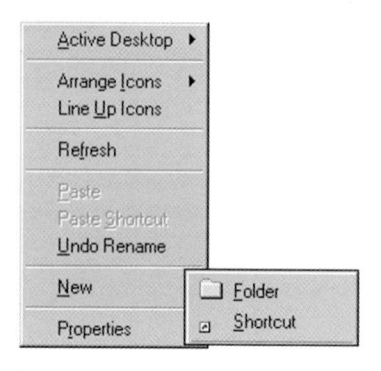

You can give new folders a name by clicking on the words 'New Folder' under the icon. Type in a name that describes how it will be used.

### Icons and shortcuts

Programs have their own icons. To get the program icon on to the desktop you need to make a 'shortcut' to the program file. There is more than one way to do this. The usual way is to:

- Right-click on the desktop.
- Left-click on the menu choice 'New'.
- Click on the menu choice 'Shortcut'.
- Type the place where the program file can be found. (This will be technical information like: C:\Programs\WinWord.exe)
- Give the icon a name: for example 'Word 97'.

*Get to this menu screen by right-clicking on the Start screen.*

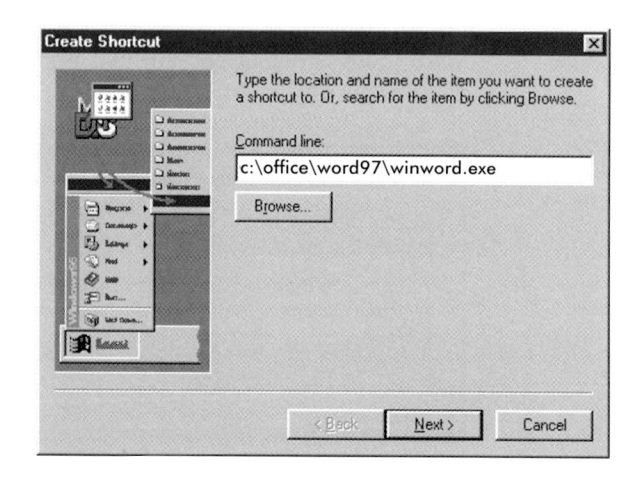

When you've made the shortcut, you can open the word-processing program Word 97 by just double-clicking on the icon.

> Continue with the computer

## SUMMARY SUMMARY SUMMARY SUMMARY SUMMARY

- Windows is a program we use to operate the computer system. It is a type of operating system.
- Windows has an easy to use, user-friendly, Graphical User Interface (GUI for short).
- On the Desktop or Start screen are icons. The icons are for programs or for folders.
- Double-clicking on an icon starts the icon's program or opens the icon's folder.
- When you open a folder, you will find it holds programs and files, and possibly even more folders.
- The Taskbar along the bottom of the screen shows you which programs are running. More than one program can be working at any one time.
- The Start button takes you to the Start menu. From this, more programs can be started, folders can be opened and Windows can be shut down.
- All windows have a Title bar; a button to close the window; a button to maximise the window; and a button to minimise the window. The 'maximise' button also turns into a restore button.
- The System menu also lets you close, maximise, minimise and restore.
- If the contents of a window are bigger than will fit in one screen then the window will have scrollbars. These let you move around the document so you can see everything.
- Clicking any word on the Menu bar provides menu choices. Click on a choice to give the computer an instruction.
- 'Shortcut keys' are a quick way to make some of the choices.
- Sometimes you need to use the *right* mouse button to get to different menu choices.
- Windows sometimes needs information, or needs to give you information. It uses a dialogue window to do this.

## Unit G: Working with Windows

### SUMMARY

- There are many choices in some dialogue windows. Make choices by scrolling through the list. Also a dialogue window often has more than one 'page'. Reach the others by clicking on the tabs at the top of the dialogue window.

- Most programs have a Help system. This can help you find out how to use the program. Click on the word Help on the Menu bar.

- Context sensitive help gives you a help screen to tell you about whatever you're doing when you ask for the help.

- New folders can be created. They hold programs and files.

- Every folder should be given a name that will tell you what is in it.

- Icons can be put on to the Desktop or Start screen by making a Shortcut.

### TASKS

1. Find out what operating system is used on any computer to which you have access. If the operating system is old, it is often not possible to run up-to-date software on that computer.

2. You may find it useful to create folders with icons on the Start screen for your main areas of work, such as schemes of work, lesson plans, notes for themes. The Start screen is also often called the Desktop. What folders do you use most often? If possible customise your Desktop.

3. Consider whether the pupils you teach need to know the skills in this unit. How are they taught them?

4. Explore the Help options on a range of programs you use or wish to use.

5. If there are programs on the computer you are using for which you would like to create shortcuts, why not try now while the unit is still fresh in your memory.

# Unit H

# Word Processing

*Books were written and printed by hand in medieval times. Now books and documents are written using computers.*

## INTRODUCTION

The first English language book to be printed using hand-set type was produced in 1477. From that point on, multiple copies of books could be printed relatively rapidly and books became more readily available. However, letters and other documents were still written by hand until the typewriter was developed in 1867. Correcting mistakes was still a problem with typewriters. It wasn't until about 1980 that computers and word-processing programs started to be used.

There are many advantages for a writer in the use of a computerised word processor. Using a word processor, you can:

- input new text.
- alter the appearance and layout of text in your document.
- cut and paste sections to change the order of the text.
- use a spell checker and a grammar checker to improve the accuracy of your work.

## Unit H: Word Processing

- align the text on the page, or put text into columns.
- outline or shade text for emphasis.
- include page numbers, headers and footers in your work.
- include graphics if you wish.
- print one or many copies of the work.

### Objectives

The objectives of this unit are to guide you through some basic word processing skills, to allow you to practise newly-developed skills and to suggest some relevant uses for these skills.

**Note:** Word-processing programs are all slightly different. Some keys or procedures mentioned here may not work exactly the same with your particular program.

*Desktop icons for 2 popular word processing programs: Microsoft Word; Wordperfect*

By the end of this chapter you will be able to:

- Use the computer to produce a text document.
- Use the computer to produce a file that is saved on the computer's hard disk, or on a floppy disk.
- Alter the appearance and layout of text.
- Print a paper copy of your document.

| | | |
|---|---|---|
| **Key words** | Document | Any piece of text. Usually quite a long piece – like a complete letter, or a whole story, or a report. Sometimes called a 'text document'. |
| | Paragraph | In word processing, any piece of text that is finished by a press of the Enter key is called a paragraph. Paragraphs can be as short as one line, or as long as an entire document. |

```
Continue with the computer
```

## SAVING AND PRINTING

It is a good idea to save work to the computer's hard disk every few minutes. Unsaved work is deleted if the computer is switched off accidentally. Some word processors have an automatic save feature which saves work regularly to ensure that nothing is lost. Once saved, the document can be re-opened if you want to use it again, or modify it. For example, standard letters to parents can be saved, and printed with a simple name change when necessary.

There are three ways to save work to the hard disk.

a) From the menu bar at the top of the screen, select File. Choose 'Save As' from the drop down menu and, in the File name box type a short name for the document. Then click on Save.

b) Another way to save work is to click on a symbol on the word processor's toolbar. The symbol might be like this on your word processor: You will then need to name the file in the manner decribed above.

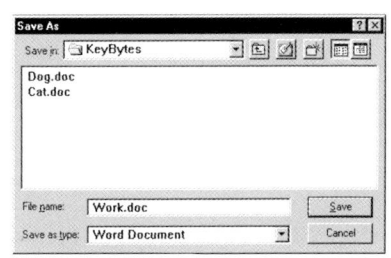

c) One other way to Save is to use CTRL and the S key together. As before, you will then be required to name your document.

Once a document has been saved and given a file name you can subsequently click on Save rather than Save As.

### Saving to a floppy disk

Although you have your document saved in a file on the computer's hard disk, it is also useful to have a copy on a floppy disk. This acts as a back-up if the original is somehow lost, and is also a way of transferring documents between computers. Ask a colleague to explain how to do this process on your machine.

### Saving to a network

Your school may allow you to save your work on a central network. Seek advice about this from your IT Co-ordinator.

### Printing

Once the work is saved, you may want a paper copy. From the menu bar at the top of the screen, select File and choose 'Print' from the drop-down menu. If everything is properly set up, simply clicking on OK will print your work.

Unit H: *Word Processing*

**How to delete and insert characters**

To correct an error in a text document:

- Use the Screen Cursor keys to position the text cursor to the left of the mistake.

- Or move the text cursor with the mouse. Click when it is in the right place.

- Use the Delete key to remove the mistake.

- Type in any character which needs to be inserted.

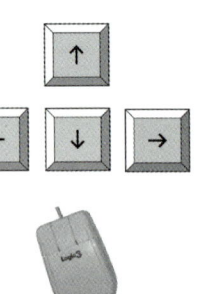

---

*Continue with the computer*

---

**PRACTICE 1**

The Atlantic salmon, *Salmo salar*, is one of the largest fish found in the British Isles and has a very interesting life cycle. The young fish known as fry hatch out in streams and spend their first year or two in fresh water. When they are larger they migrate downstream and spend a number of years at sea. Adult salmon later return to their native streams to spawn. It is during these spawning 'runs' that salmon attract the interest of fishermen and anglers. It is illegal to fish for salmon without a valid permit. They are however a highly sought after and valuable fish and attract poachers who catch and then sell them illegally. If caught by the police, poachers face a heavy fine and possible imprisonment. Unfortunately even these punishments don't seem to deter some foolish people!

*The corrected salmon story should look like this.*

## SOME USEFUL WORD PROCESSING FEATURES

### Spelling checks

Word-processor programs can check documents for spelling mistakes. These are sometimes known as spellcheckers. They can either check each word as it is typed, or check all the words when the document is finished.

*A spellchecker provides alternative spellings and words.*

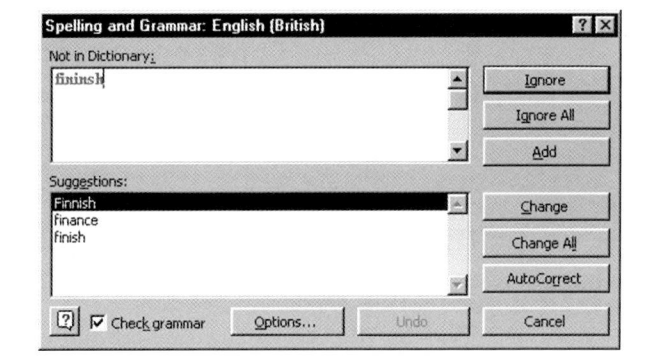

A spellchecker is a valuable tool but must be used with care. Some problems which may arise are:

1. The spellchecker may offer American spellings of words.

2. The spellchecker may not highlight mis-spellings of homophones (write/right, their/there, roll/role, etc)

## THE WORD PROCESSING KEYS

**Home** — This jumps the text cursor to the start of a line.

**End** — This jumps the text cursor to the end of a line.

**In (Insert)** — Normally, when you put the text cursor in the middle of a word and type, the new characters are inserted between other characters.

If you press the Insert key first, new characters overtype those which are already there. Pressing the Insert key again switches it off.

*Insert* is either on or off. Remember to switch it off after use.

**PgUp (Page up)** — This takes the text cursor up one page. Use this key to move towards the start of the document.

**PgDn (Page down)** — This takes the text cursor down one page. Use this key to move towards the end of the document.

The mouse can also be used to move up and down a long document.

**Scroll bar** — Clicking the arrow that points up, moves you up the document. It takes you towards the start.

Clicking on the scroll bar arrow that points down, lets you see more of the document. The arrow takes you down the document – towards the end.

Unit H: *Word Processing*

- - - - - - - - - - - - - - - - - - - - - - - -
                Continue with the computer
- - - - - - - - - - - - - - - - - - - - - - - -

## HIGHLIGHTING AND CHANGING TEXT BLOCKS

### Selecting text

Text on the screen can be highlighted (selected) to indicate to the computer that you wish to edit, move, delete or change it.

The highlighted block of text can be made **bold**, *italic* and underlined just by clicking on a button.

Once a text block is selected by highlighting you can also change the *font* (the style of the character), and the size of the characters.

> The Atlantic salmon, *Salmo salar*, is one of the largest fish found in the British Isles and has a very interesting life cycle. <mark>The young fish known as fry</mark> hatch out in streams and spend their first year or two in fresh water. When they are larger they migrate downstream and spend a number of years at sea. Adult salmon later return to their native streams to spawn.

### How to select text by highlighting

Any of the procedures outlined below can be used to highlight and select text which you may want to edit.

1. Use the Shift key and the Screen Cursor keys.

2. Click and drag the mouse over the text you want to highlight.

On many word processors:

3. Double-clicking anywhere on a word highlights the whole word.

4. Clicking at the end of a line (in the margin) highlights the whole line.

5. Three clicks on a word highlights the whole paragraph.

Check what works on the word processor you use.

Unit H: *Word Processing*

*I*
Italic

**B**
Bold

<u>U</u>
Underlined

### Why use bold, italic and underlined?
Altering the appearance of text can make your word-processed documents easier to read. Misunderstandings are minimised if text is clearly presented. This section will tell you how to change the appearance of the text.

Important words are often *italicised* or <u>underlined</u>.

Section titles are usually printed in **bold**. The size of text can also be altered for emphasis.

Text size is measured in points. The size of the letters in a font is measured in points. There are 72 points in an inch – that is, approximately 28 points per centimetre. Text on the screen is usually between 10 and 14 points. Newspaper headlines are frequently as big as 120 points or more.

M M M M M **M M M M**

*Type sizes are measured in points. These letters range from 6 points to 60 points.*

### Using changes of font
A font (originally *fount*) is a set of characters made in the same style to the same overall design. The computer provides a range of fonts. Some are ornate; others are simpler. Some have letters with serifs (small flat 'feet') which make them easier to read because they visually link with one another into words. Different fonts are appropriate for different documents. A general rule is that too many changes of font style within a document can be unhelpful: the reader starts to concentrate on the medium rather than the message.

Unit L of *KeyBytes* tells you more about this.

*Highlight the text then choose the name of the font you want to use. There are thousands of different fonts: here are a few.*

This font is Times
This font is Courier
This font is Helvetica
This font is Kids
*This font is Kaufmann*

> Continue with the computer

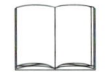

## CUT, COPY, PASTE AND DELETE

Word processors let you move any *text block*, or make a copy of it, or delete it completely. To do any of these things highlight a section of text, then choose:

Clicking on the **Cut** button takes the text block out of the document and stores it in the computer's internal memory.

The **Copy** button copies the text block into the computer's internal memory without taking it out of the document.

The ***Paste button*** allows you to reuse the text block that you have just cut or copied. The text block can go in somewhere else. Click the mouse to put the text cursor where you want the piece of text to go. Then click on the Paste button. This is called pasting!

If you press the ***Delete key*** when a text block is highlighted the text is deleted, without a copy being kept.

However if you delete text and then change your mind, you can immediately click on the menu-bar heading Edit. In the menu you will find 'Undo'. Click on Undo and the last deleted text block will re-appear.

### Shortcut keys

It is possible to use the keyboard instead of the buttons to cut, copy and paste. Working with highlighted text, the following combinations of keys will carry out these operations:

|  |  |
|---|---|
| *Cut* | Ctrl and X keys together |
| *Copy* | Ctrl and C keys together |
| *Paste* | Ctrl and V keys together |

More useful shortcut keys:

|  |  |
|---|---|
| *Ctrl A* | selects (highlights) the entire document |
| *Ctrl B* | makes the selected text bold |
| *Ctrl I* | makes the selected text italic |
| *Ctrl U* | underlines the selected text |
| *Ctrl S* | saves the document |
| *Ctrl P* | prints the document |
| *Ctrl Q* | quits or exits from the current document |

Unit H: *Word Processing*

> **Continue with the computer**

## MARGINS AND ALIGNMENT

When you start a new document think about the margins and the text alignment.

The margins are the spaces at either side of the text (and also above the text, and below the text). A good choice of margins and text alignment can help to make documents neat and easy to read.

In this book the margin is 15 mm on the left and on the right. The main text is 'left-aligned' (which leaves a jagged margin on the right).

When you are word processing any paragraph you type can be left-aligned, right-aligned, centred or fully aligned (also called justified or fully justified).

Thirty days hath September, April, June and November. All the rest have thirty-one, excepting February alone, which has twenty-eight days clear and twenty-nine in each leap year.

*This is left-aligned text*

*This is right-aligned text*

Thirty days hath September, April, June and November. All the rest have thirty-one, excepting February alone, which has twenty-eight days clear and twenty-nine in each leap year.

Thirty days hath September, April, June and November. All the rest have thirty-one, excepting February alone, which has twenty-eight days clear and twenty-nine in each leap year.

*This is centred text*

*This is fully aligned text (also called justified or fully justified)*

Thirty days hath September, April, June and November. All the rest have    thirty-one,    excepting February alone, which has twenty-eight days clear and twenty-nine in each leap year.

Unit H: *Word Processing*

## OPEN, SEARCH AND REPLACE

### Open files

Document files on your hard disk can be opened and changes made to them.

The way to open files is the same in almost every program. Click on the menu heading File, then click on Open, then choose the text data file you want.

Another way to do this is to click on a symbol on the word processor's toolbar. The symbol might be like this on your word processor:

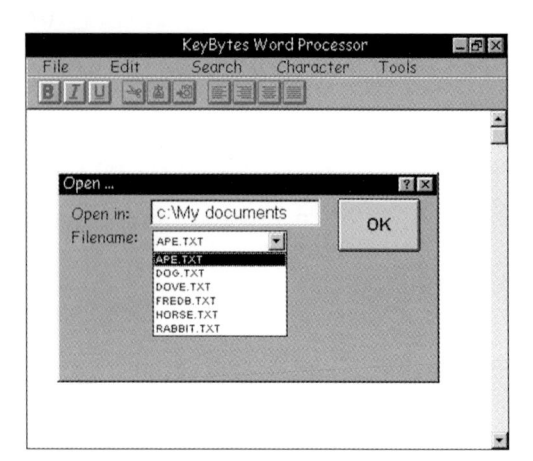

### Search and Search-and-Replace

Word processors can be made to search automatically for words or other data. Just type in the words (or word, or any other data) you want to find. The word processor starts a search. The search stops as soon as it finds the data.

You can also automatically replace data found by the search. For example you could search for 'Jan 2001' and replace it with 'Oct 2002'. Or replace it with anything else you like using as many words as you need. This is called *Search and Replace*.

*Search and Replace in action on the KeyBytes program.*

Unit H: *Word Processing*

```
┌─────────────────────────────────────────────┐
│         Continue with the computer          │
└─────────────────────────────────────────────┘
```

## WORD PROCESSING AT WORK

There are a few different word processing programs on sale. Well-known programs include Microsoft Word and Corel WordPerfect. Find out which word processing program your school or college uses.

Your word processor will probably do many more things than you have practised in *KeyBytes: Word Processing*. Put aside some time to look at all the options available on your school or college word processor. Do this by clicking all the buttons on the 'menu bar' and exploring the choices they offer. We'll mention a few of the most common features here:

**1.** *Mail merge.* Companies often send a copy of the same letter addressed to thousands of different people at the same time. They use mail merge to 'merge' each person's address with the same word-processed letter. (You'll find out more about this in Unit J of *KeyBytes*.)

**2.** You can easily create *Tables* in a document. It's usual to be able to select the thickness of the lines between the columns, the width of each column, the number of rows, etc.

**3.** Most word processors let you write your own small programs to do special word-processing jobs. Sometimes these can be simply to save you typing the same thing over and over (for instance your own name). They are called *Macros*.

**4.** *Drawing program.* Simple drawings can be made with some word-processing programs and used in the document. Also drawings or scanned photographs made in other programs can be *imported* into word-processed documents.

**5.** Sometimes you might want to use *Numbered headings* – like

> *3.1 The KeyBytes Word Processor*
> *3.2 Opening a File*
> *3.3 Saving a File*
> *3.4 Closing a File*

If you add new text or make corrections to the document the headings might need to go in a different order. Then all the numbers will need to be changed. Some word processors will change all the numbers automatically.

**6.** You can make paragraph *Styles*. For example you could create a style called 'Heading' for all the big bold headings in your document and another style called 'Normal Text' for the ordinary paragraphs. That makes it quick and easy to change the text.

Unit H: Word Processing

7. The *Internet* needs word-processed text to be put into a special 'code' called HTML. Word processing programs can save documents using HTML so that it can be used on the Internet.

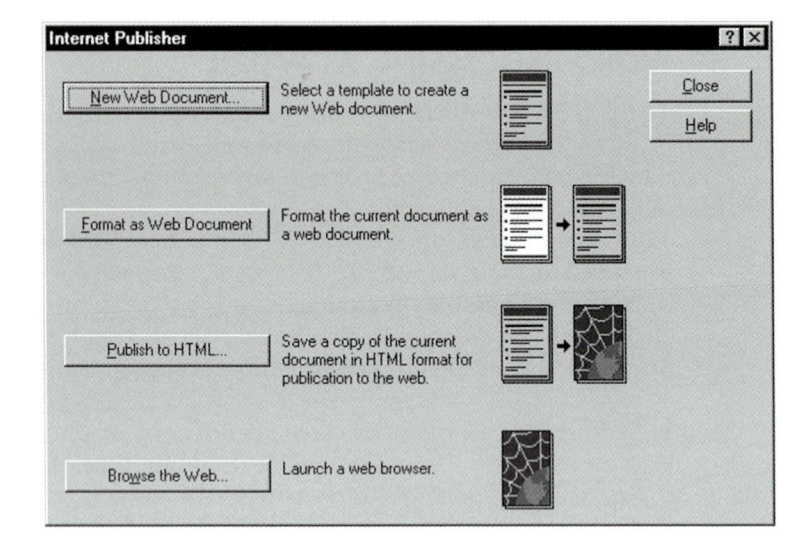

*The HTML conversion screen from Corel Wordperfect 7*

```
Continue with the computer
```

## SUMMARY  SUMMARY  SUMMARY  SUMMARY  SUMMARY

- Using a computer to write is called word processing.
- With word processing you can easily correct errors and format documents.
- Word-processed documents should be given a name and saved as a file. Use Save As... on the File menu.
- Save the document every few minutes so nothing much will be lost if the power goes off.
- A spellchecker can be used to check the spelling in a document.
- The Home key jumps the text cursor to the beginning of a line and the End key jumps the text cursor to the end of a line.
- The Page Up and Page Down keys are used to go up or down a page.

## Unit H: Word Processing

## Summary

- You can use the mouse and scroll bar to move up and down a document.
- The Insert key switches 'overwriting' on and off.
- To highlight (select) a text block, click and drag the mouse, or use the Shift key with a Screen Cursor key.
- Highlighted text can be made **bold**, *italic* or <u>underlined</u> to make the selected block of text stand out from the normal text.
- A character in one font usually looks different from the same character in another font.
- Different type sizes can be used as well as changes of font.
- You can cut, copy and paste or delete any text block.
- Shortcut keys can be used instead of the cut, copy and paste buttons.
- The spaces on the sides of the page are called margins.
- Paragraphs can be left-aligned, right-aligned, fully aligned or centred.
- You can search for words in a document and replace them with other words.
- Some word processors do lots of useful things, like: mail merge, tables, macros, drawing, paragraph styles, numbered headings and Internet coding.

**TASK** Using a word processor at school or home, compile a worksheet or other document that you would find useful in your classroom. Experiment with the layout using the ideas in this unit, e.g. font, type size, bold, italic. Pages 161–167 will explain how to make 'interactive' electronic worksheets which use material from the Internet.

# Unit 1

# Spreadsheets

## INTRODUCTION

When personal computers first became a practical tool, it was the spreadsheet that was most important for many users; especially those in business and industry. Spreadsheets can hold large amounts of information and the programs perform complex calculations very quickly. The information can be displayed in a variety of ways.

Schools often use commercially available spreadsheets, such as Excel, but may also use specialist programs to assist in financial administration and monitoring pupil achievement. You may have seen other uses of spreadsheets in your school or college to give information to parents, manage finances or record and organise examination results.

### Objectives

In this unit we are going to look at how to use a spreadsheet to perform calculations. We will look at some of the benefits of spreadsheets and use the spreadsheet to try out a number of calculations. The object of this unit is to provide an introduction to the major features of spreadsheets and give opportunities to practise some tasks using a spreadsheet program.

By the end of this unit you will:
- be familiar with the layout of spreadsheets.
- be able to make calculations and use formulas.
- be able to convert spreadsheet data to a graphical form.

Unit I: *Spreadsheets*

```
Spreadsheet - (KeyBytes)                    _ □ X
File    Edit    View    Insert    Tools
A2  Sandwich                          >>  ><  <<  B
```

|   | A | B | C | D |
|---|---|---|---|---|
| 1 | FOOD | PRICE (£) | QUANTITY | TOTAL (£) |
| 2 | Sandwich | 1.50 | 155 | 232.50 |
| 3 | Baguette | 1.80 | 112 | 201.60 |
| 4 | Jacket potato | 1.95 | 90 | 175.50 |
| 5 | Pizza slice | 1.75 | 18 | 31.50 |
| 6 |   |   |   |   |
| 7 |   |   |   |   |
| 8 |   |   |   |   |

**Key words**

**Layout**    The position of words and numbers in a spreadsheet.

**Active cell**    Cell into which data can be typed.

**Active area**    Area under the spreadsheet menu bar which can be used for entering data.

**Modelling**    Using a spreadsheet to test the effects of different data.

```
Continue with the computer
```

**PRACTICE 1**

This exercise gives you a first opportunity to use a spreadsheet and demonstrates the speed and accuracy of calculations performed on a spreadsheet.

You may need a calculator for the first part of each exercise.

| Name | Sandwiches | Baguettes | Jacket potatoes | Pizza slices |
|---|---|---|---|---|
| Price | £1.50 | £1.80 | £1.95 | £1.75 |
| Jemima | 1 | 2 | 3 | 0 |
| John | 2 | 3 | 1 | 2 |
| Annette | 2 | 1 | 1 | 1 |
| Gordon | 5 | 4 | 3 | 2 |
| Lianne | 2 | 6 | 0 | 0 |

## A CLOSER LOOK AT THE SPREADSHEET

A spreadsheet is made up of *cells* (the boxes that data is typed into).

In any spreadsheet the highlighted cell is the *active cell*. You can instantly change the active cell by clicking on another cell or by using the Screen Cursor keys to move around the spreadsheet. Data can be typed into the active cell.

As well as an active cell there is also an *active area* under the menu bar. Active cell data can also be entered here – and this area always shows what is in the active cell.

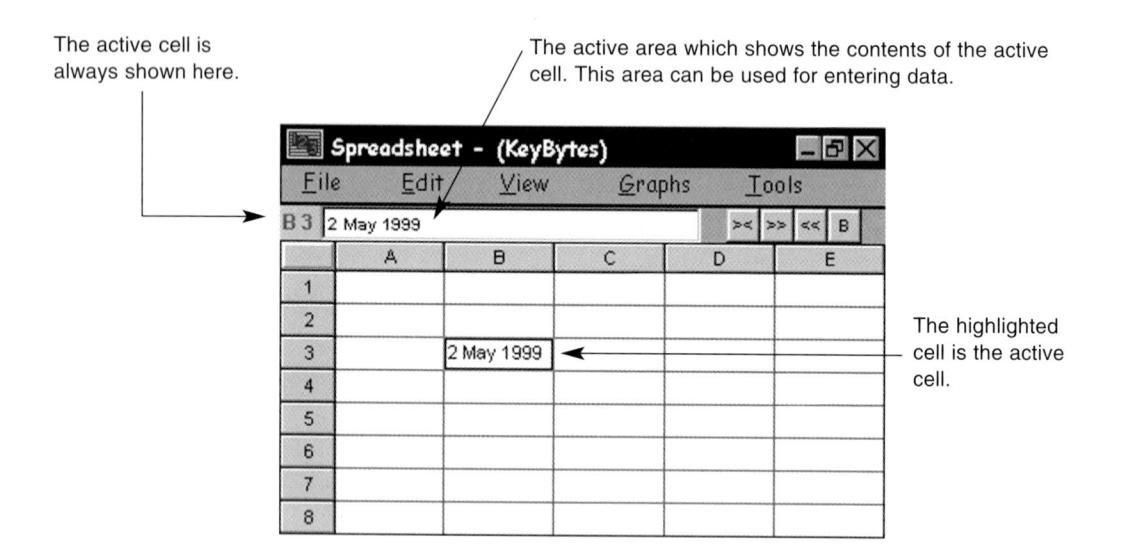

The active cell is always shown here.

The active area which shows the contents of the active cell. This area can be used for entering data.

The highlighted cell is the active cell.

*Data can be typed into the active cell (or into the active area)*

The cells which go across the spreadsheet are a *row*.

The cells which are stacked on top of each other are a *column*.

Each row, column and cell has a name.

- Rows are named by a *number*, for example: row 1 or row 2.
- Columns are named by a *letter*, for example: column A or column B.
- Cells are named using their column letter and their row number, for example: cell A1 or cell B2.

The cell name example you can see in the picture is:

**Cell A6** (the cell is positioned where column A and row 6 meet).

Every cell can hold data. The data can be numeric (numbers) or alphabetic (letters and words). Some of that data will be formulas – but more about that later in the unit.

A spreadsheet of 5 columns and 5 rows contains $5 \times 5 = 25$ cells; one with 25 columns and 100 rows contains $25 \times 100 = 2500$ cells.

The number of columns and rows used can be very big: hundreds of columns and thousands of rows!

```
Continue with the computer
```

Unit I: *Spreadsheets*

## THE LAYOUT OF A SPREADSHEET

Good spreadsheet layout is important. Even complicated spreadsheets can be easy to read if they are carefully laid out.

*Click, then drag the 'tool tip' to make a column wider or narrower*

*Column widths can be adjusted by using the 'tool tip'.*

You can make the columns *wider*.

The characters can be large or small; or **bold** or *italic*.

The data in any cell can be centred, left-aligned or right-aligned.

None of the layout options affects the way the program calculates.

*Different spreadsheet programs use different symbols for alignment. Here are some common alignment symbols.*

Left-align symbol     Centring symbol     Right-align symbol

Spreadsheets can be set up so that special layout instructions can apply to the whole spreadsheet, or only to selected columns, rows or cells. For instance you can give instructions to:

- show all the data as whole numbers (without decimal points);

- always show numbers to two decimal points (or more);
- put a % sign after every number in a selected column;
- put a £ sign in front of every number in a selected row.

```
Continue with the computer
```

**PRACTICE 2** The spreadsheet shows Millie's sandwich bar's weekly sales and profits. Some of the data has already been filled in. You must fill in the missing data. It's shown in the table below.

When you enter each of the numbers watch the spreadsheet do the profit calculations.

| A | B | C | D | E |
|---|---|---|---|---|
| Food | Number Sold | Buy at (£) | Sell at (£) | Profit (£) |
| Sandwiches | 140 | 0.70 | 1.50 | |
| Baguettes | 100 | 0.95 | 1.80 | |
| Jacket potatoes | 100 | 1.05 | 1.95 | |
| Pizza slices | 40 | 0.85 | 1.75 | |
| | | | Total | |

The price they 'Sell at', minus the cost they 'Buy at' gives the profit on one item. So

(Sell at) − (Buy at) = (Profit £)

Therefore for each row the spreadsheet calculation is:

Column D − Column C = Column E

```
Continue with the computer
```

Unit I: *Spreadsheets*

## USING FORMULAS

Spreadsheets use formulas to carry out calculations. These formulas use an 'arithmetical operator' (plus, minus, divide, etc) in addition to cell names (and sometimes numbers). Every formula starts with a sign which indicates to the program that it must perform a calculation. *KeyBytes*, and many other spreadsheet programs, use the = sign for this.

Formulas use *cell names* with plus, minus, divide, etc.

For example, if you want to add a number in cell A1 to a number in cell A2, you would type in =A1+A2.

Formulas are used to add, subtract, multiply and divide. A few examples are shown below:

=A1+A4        (Add the contents of cell A1 to the contents of cell A4)

=A4–B9        (Subtract the contents of cell B9 from the contents of cell A4)

=C4*E9        (Multiply the contents of cell C4 by the contents of cell E9. *Note:* To multiply you have to use the * instead of the ×)

=B5/B7        (Divide the contents of cell B5 by the contents of cell B7. *Note:* To divide you have to use the forward slash / instead of ÷)

Usually you can only see the formula in its spreadsheet cell while it is being typed in. Then – it sits hidden – 'waiting to pounce'. Nothing happens until some data is entered into the cells referred to in the formula. Then the formula goes into action!

But even if it's hidden, you can always see the formula again by highlighting its cell. Then look at the active area at the top of the spreadsheet. The hidden formula can be seen in the active area.

### Copying formulas

There's one trick that makes it very quick to work with spreadsheets. Once you have worked out a formula which gives the answer for one column or row, it can be copied to another. The formula alters itself.

For example: one cell in every row might need dividing by another cell in the same row (=C2/C4) – and the answer put into a third cell (C6).

Instead of typing another formula into cell D6 to do the same calculation for row D – copy the formula from C6.

So: =C2/C4    becomes    =D2/D4.

You practised this in the program.

*A formula can be copied from one cell to other cells.*

| | A | B | C | D |
|---|---|---|---|---|
| 1 | FOOD | PRICE (£) | QUANTITY | TOTAL (£) |
| 2 | Sandwich | 1.50 | 155 | 232.50 |
| 3 | Baguette | 1.80 | 112 | |
| 4 | Jacket potato | 1.95 | 90 | |
| 5 | Pizza slice | 1.75 | 18 | |
| 6 | | | | |
| 7 | | | | |
| 8 | | | | |

D2 =B2*C2

## More advanced work with formulas

In addition to the simple calculations based on the contents of existing cells, more complicated combined calculations are also possible. The important thing to remember when setting up the formulas is that the computer always works out the calculation that is inside the brackets first. Then performs the calculation which is outside the brackets. For example:

=(A2+10)*3    means add 10 to the number in cell A2, then multiply that new number by 3.

=(B4–B5)/10    means subtract the number in cell B5 from the number in cell B4, then divide the answer by 10.

Sometimes you might need even more sophisticated calculations – but the approach should be just the same.

=(D5+10)/(A3–B4)*100 is easy on a spreadsheet.

```
Continue with the computer
```

Unit I: *Spreadsheets*

## COMMON CALCULATIONS

There are several calculations which are used very often.

Adding up a row or column is one of these often-used calculations. It can be done in two ways. For example:

=A1+A2+A3+A4+A5+A6

or much more quickly

=SUM(A1:A6)

The parts of the formula **=SUM(A1:A6)** are:

=          Tells the spreadsheet a formula follows.

**SUM**     Tells the spreadsheet to add up the contents of all the cells that follow.

**(A1:A6)** Identifies all the cells from cell A1 to cell A6.

The SUM formula (or 'SUM function') is the most useful of many. You will need to look at the manual for the spreadsheet your school uses to find out others that are possible. You will probably find some others that will be helpful.

### Toolbar buttons

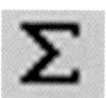

=SUM is so useful that some spreadsheet programs give it a symbol and a button on the Toolbar. The symbol is $\Sigma$ which is a Greek letter called 'sigma'.

Here are two other formulas that are especially useful. Like =SUM they sometimes have a symbol and a button on the Toolbar.

**=AVG(B1:B100)**        Will give the 'average of all the numbers' contained in cells B1 to cell B100.

**=COUNT(C1:C1000)**    This counts how many cells hold data: between cell C1 and cell C1000.

The method for use of the Toolbar buttons can vary from one spreadsheet program to another – but generally it is:

- Highlight the range of cells which hold the data;
- Extend the highlighting to encompass the cell you want to hold the answer (this will become the active formula cell);
- Click on the function button.

Unit I: Spreadsheets

The answer appears in the active formula cell – without further work. So it saves you typing the formula.

You'll need to learn exactly how to do this for whichever spreadsheet program you use. But it's worth learning – it's much quicker than typing!

### Adding columns or rows

One feature of spreadsheets that is particularly useful is the facility to add or remove rows and columns. This allows additional data to be added at any time, without losing the existing information.

You can highlight a column on your spreadsheet, and then use the Insert menu to add a column.

The same can be done for rows.

```
Continue with the computer
```

## WHAT IF?

An important use of spreadsheets is to look at possible outcomes when conditions change. For example, using a spreadsheet of class marks, you could consider the effect of one child improving his or her marks in the next piece of work, or of all children making an improvement, or to judge the effect of altering the grading system.

Spreadsheets are used extensively to help determine budgets in schools. It is possible to work from existing data and add new information or change data to see what the overall effect would be.

You can try this by adding a new column or row of marks to a spreadsheet of class marks and looking at the effect of different scores on the class or pupil average.

| | A | B | C | D |
|---|---|---|---|---|
| 1 | FOOD | PRICE (£) | QUANTITY | TOTAL (£) |
| 2 | Sandwich | 1.50 | 155 | 232.50 |
| 3 | Baguette | 1.80 | 112 | 201.60 |
| 4 | Jacket potato | 1.95 | 90 | 175.50 |
| 5 | Pizza slice | 1.75 | 18 | 31.50 |
| 6 | | | | |
| 7 | | | | |
| 8 | | | | |

In the KeyBytes program we saw 'what would happen if' some changes were made. What if the bar sold more pizza? What if we put the price of baguettes up?, etc.

Unit I: *Spreadsheets*

Using spreadsheets in this way is often called modelling – looking at future scenarios using possible future data.

Remember though that it is vitally important that any modelling is done with all the facts clear. You may set yourself the target of raising average scores for a class to such an extent that the individual targets for pupils become unrealistic.

> Continue with the computer

## WHAT ELSE CAN A SPREADSHEET DO?

You have seen that a spreadsheet can calculate very quickly using formulas, and can be set up with a good layout which makes it easy to read. The information in a spreadsheet can be used in many ways.

Spreadsheets:
- can be printed onto paper;
- can use colour to highlight critical data;
- can be turned into graphs which visually show the total figures;
- these graphs can also be printed – in colour if you have the equipment.

Different types of graph are possible. Often one type of graph will show a set of results more clearly than another type of graph. It is very easy to change from one graph to another. Usually a few clicks of the mouse on the spreadsheet menu or on the spreadsheet buttons is all that is needed.

Graphs of spreadsheet totals are usually very clear and useful to other people because the results are so interestingly illustrated.

You could try the different graphing or chart options to present the data from a class marks spreadsheet in a variety of ways. You may consider which are the most effective presentations of the information.

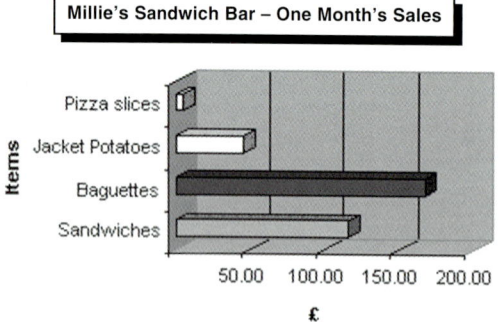

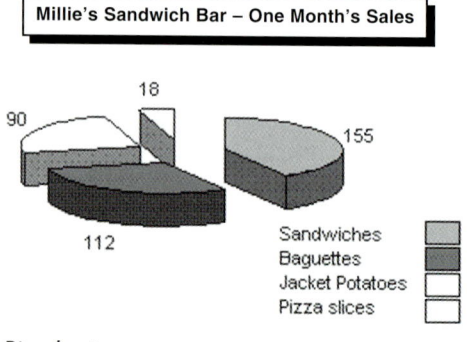

*Bar chart*

*Pie chart*

Unit 1: *Spreadsheets*

> Continue with the computer

## SPREADSHEETS – A POWERFUL AND FLEXIBLE TOOL

Spreadsheets are a powerful and flexible tool that can be used in a variety of situations to provide answers, explore change and present results. They allow anyone who can deploy simple arithmetical logic to perform a range of sometimes complex calculations quickly, easily and accurately.

Another advantage of electronic spreadsheets is that once a spreadsheet has been set up correctly new data can be easily added and new results explored.

## SUMMARY SUMMARY SUMMARY SUMMARY SUMMARY

- Spreadsheets enable very fast and accurate calculations to be carried out.
- A spreadsheet is made up of cells. The cells are in columns and rows.
- Columns are cells stacked on top of each other. Each column is named with a letter. For example: column C.
- Rows are cells arranged next to each other across the spreadsheet. Each row is named with a number. For example: row 3.
- Each cell has a name. It is made up from its column letter and its row number. For example: cell B5.
- Each cell can hold numeric or other data.
- Good layout is important. It makes the data easier to understand.
- Spreadsheet calculations are done using formulas.
- Some examples of formulas are:

    =A1+A6   (Add the contents of cell A6 to the contents of cell A1)
    =B3–B4   (Subtract the contents of cell B4 from the contents of cell B3)
    C4*C8    (Multiply the contents of cell C4 by the contents of cell C8)
    B5/A5    (Divide the contents of cell B5 by the contents of cell A5)

Unit I: *Spreadsheets*

## SUMMARY

- Columns or rows of data can be added together using a =SUM formula. For example: =SUM(B1:B15)
- Once formulas have been put into a spreadsheet it is easy to try lots of 'What if?' calculations.
- Modelling, or 'What if?', calculations are where different numbers are tried in a calculation to see what the effect of the change would be.
- Spreadsheets can easily be turned into graphs.
- The spreadsheets or graphs can be in colour and can be printed on any type of printer.
- Spreadsheets have enabled a wide range of people to carry out calculations quickly, easily and accurately.

## TASKS

1. For this task you will need to use whichever spreadsheet program is available on your PC (this may be Excel or Quatro Pro or another similar program).

   Set up a simple spreadsheet to record marks for a small number of pupils who have taken a test each week for the previous six weeks. Enter a mark against each pupil for each of the six tests. Use the SUM and AVG functions to work out the total number of marks for each child, the average mark for each child and the average mark for the class.

2. You should now consider the possible uses of spreadsheets for your classroom. The collection and manipulation of scientific or mathematical data would seem obvious, but other subject areas may also benefit from the use of a spreadsheet. Any situation in which children need to manipulate data may offer opportunities for the use of a spreadsheet program. As with other applications, the choice of appropriate technology for the task should be a key consideration at all times.

# Unit J
## Databases

### INTRODUCTION

Computerised databases are an effective way of creating and maintaining records. Much information can be stored in, and retrieved from, a database. One of the advantages of computer databases is the speed with which relevant information can be located. Databases are used in libraries, for medical purposes, to keep track of stock in the retail trade, and, in schools, to collect information about pupils in a way that is useful and accessible. Schools can use databases of student records to track students' progress – identifying those who are not achieving what is expected of them.

### Objectives

In this unit we are going to practise working with a database and then construct and use another database.

By the end of this unit you will:
- understand the purposes of storing information in computerised databases.
- enter and edit database information.
- use a database to locate relevant information.
- construct a new database using a 'wizard'.

**Key words**

| | |
|---|---|
| Data | A term for information of any kind. Data can be alphabetic or numeric. |
| Database | A system for storage and retrieval of data. |
| Field | A specific item of information or data. |
| Sort | To arrange information according to different criteria. |

Unit J: Databases

## WHY USE A DATABASE?

Databases are used for record-keeping.

Computerised databases replace the paper-based systems that have been traditionally used in schools, by doctors, by libraries, and so on.

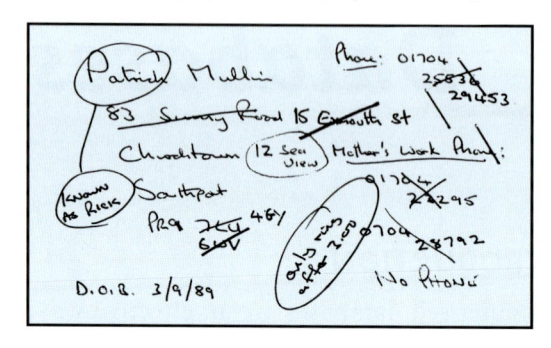

A comparison of the two methods is given in the following table.

| Paper-based Record Keeping | Computer Database |
| --- | --- |
| Completing cards or folders is time consuming | Entering information is relatively straightforward |
| The cards or folders could be difficult to read | The typed text is always legible |
| The paper or card could get worn and damaged | Files can be damaged, but keeping a copy is easy |
| Locating the relevant information could be problematic | Locating information is relatively straightforward |
| Large amounts of stored information are unwieldy | Large amounts of stored information are unproblematic |
| Files and cards could be lost irretrievably | Files and cards can be lost – but copies can be kept |
| Security is a problem | Security is a problem |

Each *record* in a database stores information. A database can have hundreds of thousands of records – even millions. Every database record is split up into *fields*. Each field has a heading which indicates the data it contains.

The *field headings are the same* in every record in a database, but the *data in the fields* can be different in every record.

By searching the database, all records that contain the data you wish to use can be found. Database records can be easily updated and they can be sorted into different orders.

Unit J: *Databases*

*A database record showing 6 fields and their headings.*

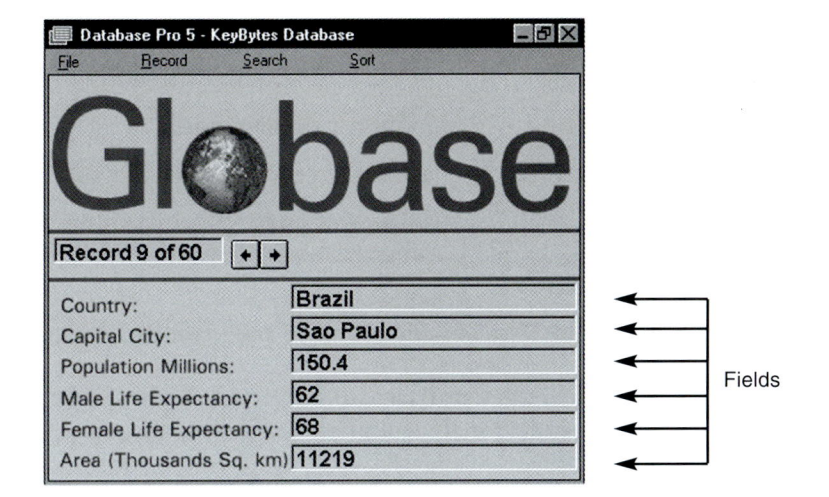

**Database Pro 5 - KeyBytes Database**
File   Record   Search   Sort

# Globase

Record 9 of 60

| Country: | Brazil |
| Capital City: | Sao Paulo |
| Population Millions: | 150.4 |
| Male Life Expectancy: | 62 |
| Female Life Expectancy: | 68 |
| Area (Thousands Sq. km) | 11219 |

Fields

---
**Continue with the computer**
---

**PRACTICE 1**

Use 'Globase' on the screen and a combination of the techniques you have learned, to find the answers to the following questions:

a) What is the capital of Cameroon?

b) Which country in 'Globase' has the smallest population?

c) What is the female life expectancy in Holland?

d) What is the area of Japan?

e) In which country is male life expectancy shortest?

f) Where do women live longest?

g) Is Dakar a country?

---
**Continue with the computer**
---

## USING A DATABASE

### Searching and sorting

Each database record contains a number of fields. The fields are the specific items of data to be recorded. There can be several fields in a record. The database enables you to locate any record, or any data in any field.

Using a database, it is possible to carry out the following operations:

- Sort the records in the database in different ways.
- Search the database for a single record.
- Search the database for several records all containing the same data.
- Look through records you have found in a number of different ways; for example by using the arrow keys, the 'Next' button or by using 'Go To'.
- Use the 'Go To' command to take you to any known record number.

Records in the database can be sorted. They can be arranged into another order, such as alphabetical, size, age, etc.

One database search (or sort) can be linked to another. For example, a linked search will answer such questions as: 'Which country has the smallest population per square kilometre of land?'

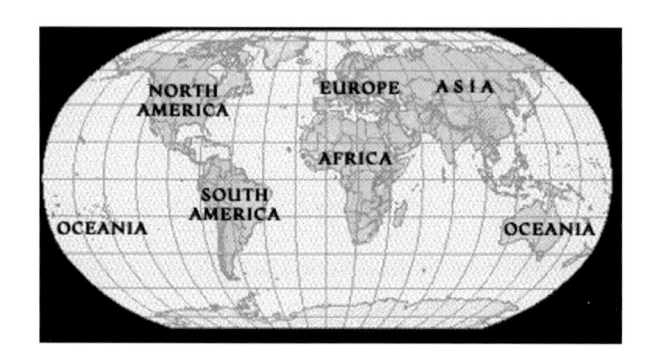

### Setting up a new database

Before any work is done at the computer, the following questions need to be considered:

- What information do you want?
- How will you get that information?
- What order should it be in on the database records?
- What is a short and clear field heading for each?
- Will each field store alphabetical data (text), or numbers, or mixed text and numbers?

Once you have decided upon the answers to these questions, you can set about creating your own database. Most database programs have a 'wizard'. This will assist you in the creation of a database, by giving on-screen instructions.

Unit J: *Databases*

*Microsoft Works Database Wizard*

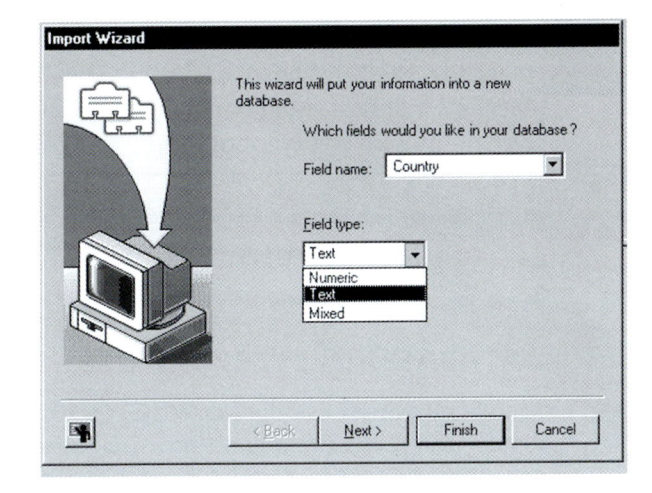

---

**Continue with the computer**

---

**PRACTICE 2**

Use 'Clubbase' on the screen to find the answers to the following:

**Don't forget:** Use 'Go To...' in the Search menu to find a record number.

Click on 'Search' in the Search menu and enter any word you need.

Use the 'Sort' menu to put the records into order.

After 'Sort' you can use 'Go To...' to find the record you need.

a) Which member of the club lives in Cardiff?

b) Who has membership number 0030?

c) If the members' names are put into alphabetical order whose name is first, and whose name is last?

d) How many club members live in England?

e) Which members say their interest is mountain biking?

f) Whose interest is rock climbing?

g) Gillian Rogers was the last person to join. What is her membership number?

---

**Continue with the computer**

Unit J: Databases

**PRACTICE 3** — The program offers you the opportunity to practise adding a new record to the 'Clubbase' database. The details of the new member are: Martin Lindhurst; Membership Number 0044; Northampton, England. E-mail: mlindhurst@abbots.sch.uk Main interest: Karate.

*Continue with the computer*

## DATABASES IN EVERYDAY USE

Many companies use databases to store names, addresses and other details about customers and potential customers. Schools and colleges can similarly record details of parents of their students. This simplifies sending letters to every person who has a record in the database.

Adding names and addresses to a standard letter is called 'mail merge'. The letter is typed in a word processor once. Special characters are typed where the name and address are to be placed. The letter is then 'merged' with each person's address from his or her record in the database. This is how standard letters, individually addressed, are produced.

### The School
Stamford
PB8 1LL

23 October 200…

Mr & Mrs Welsh
12 Station Lane
Stamford
PB16 2ZX

Dear Mr & Mrs Welsh

As part of our topic work this term, we have been studying 'The Ancient Greeks'. We have arranged a visit to The British Museum so that we can look at authentic artefacts, such as pottery and jewellery.

The visit will take place on 25th July. We will leave school at 8.30 a.m. and return at 6 p.m. Please complete the enclosed form to give your permission for your child to take part in this visit.

Yours sincerely


K Marsh
(Head Teacher)

### Databases and legislation

You will probably be aware that data protection legislation exists. This applies to schools and colleges just as much as to businesses. Before storing details of individuals on databases at school, check that you comply with the law. The Data Protection Commissioner's web site is at www.dataprotection.gov.uk.

> Continue with the computer

### WHOSE MISTAKE?

Databases contain a lot of information and most of it will have been typed in. Typing mistakes are easily made. For example, one parent may have two records in the database. Addresses and other information may be factually inaccurate. In addition, the technical people who work on the database program can make mistakes. These types of mistakes are due to 'human error'. The computer can neither detect nor correct such errors, therefore accurate input is extremely important.

## Computer Error Provides 4 Week Holiday

Manchester – A 17 year old girl used a fault in her Bank's computer to take a holiday.

When she took out a small amount of cash on 5 December Rachel Jones overheard the staff saying that the Bank's main computer was not working. Rachel tried the cash machine outside the Bank and found it was still working. Then she went to nine other branches of the bank and took out a total of £4,500.

She used this money to take a four week luxury holiday in Majorca. In the meantime the bank had discovered that Rachel had taken the money and reported the incident to the police. They were waiting for her when she returned from Majorca!

## Murderer Let Free By Computer Error

Antwerp – Because her name was entered wrongly in the computer controlled 'Wanted List', the German police allowed the 34 year old Marianne Olem to enter Germany and disappear.

As a result of this error she was not stopped at passport control. Her partner, the 47 year old Belgian, August de Blaue was stopped and arrested by the German police. He has since admitted to killing 44 year old Gustav Weimoetsch along with Olem.

The Belgian authorities have asked the German authorities to return August de Blaue for trial. Marianne Olem still cannot be traced.

## Unit J: Databases

> Continue with the computer

## SUMMARY SUMMARY SUMMARY SUMMARY SUMMARY

- A set of data records is called a database.
- Each record contains data that is linked, for example, information about a student.
- Different pieces of data are stored in different fields, for example, one field for name, another for age, etc.
- Records can be scrolled through until you find the one you want, but that is a slow process.
- You can search very quickly for any word, in any field, using 'Search' and 'Go To'.
- Searches often find more than one record with similar data. Use 'Next' or click through these records to find the one you want.
- Putting the records into order is called sorting.
- Alphabetical order is often used to sort names.
- Numbers can be sorted in order, with the largest number in the first or last position, according to preference.
- Field headings must be decided before you can create a new database.
- Decide what type of data is needed in each field: text, numbers, mixed, etc.
- A wizard can be used to help design and create the new database.
- New records can be added, and existing records can be changed, or deleted.
- Mail merge is where database records are merged with a word-processed letter. The same letter can then be sent to many different people without further work.
- Database details can easily be printed onto labels as well as letters.
- Humans make errors and incorrect data can be input by mistake.
- The improper use of databases is against the law.

Unit J: *Databases*

**TASKS**

1. Find out what database packages are used in your school. The departments you will find these in might include History, when census databases are used; and Administration where records on pupils are kept.

2. Consider what uses of databases can apply to your subject area. Take steps to ensure you use them appropriately.

# Unit K

# Graphics

## INTRODUCTION

The development of computer technology has made it possible to generate high quality images for use in a variety of fields. There are many examples of this, from pictures drawn for adverts, to circuit diagrams and technical drawings produced by engineers. Some programs allow you to manipulate images from other sources, such as digital cameras or scanners.

A picture or a drawing produced or displayed on a computer is called a graphic.

*Web pages make lots of use of graphics.*

### Objectives

In this unit you will use a simple drawing program and learn about aspects of graphics programs that are available for use in schools.

By the end of this unit you will:

- know the basics of how to draw using the computer.
- know how to use libraries of artwork ('clipart').
- be able to use the skills you learn, with drawing programs that you may use in the future.

## Unit K: Graphics

**Key words**

**CAD** — An abbreviation for computer-aided design.

**CAM** — An abbreviation for computer-aided manufacture.

**Clipart** — An illustration that has been created to be included in a library or libraries of images.

**Graphic** — An illustration or image, usually created with the aid of a computer.

**Package** — A term that is often used to describe any substantial computer program that enables its user to create something or carry out a series of complex processes.

**File formats** — Graphics files can be stored in several different ways. Some take up more disk space than others or have other varying properties. The 'file format' is shown by the three character extension following the name of the file. For example Cartoon.bmp shows the drawing has been saved in a 'bitmap' file format.

```
Continue with the computer
```

### LEARNING TO DRAW

Drawing programs offer a range of *tools* that you can use to draw, colour or embellish graphics in a number of ways.

The *Freehand* tool allows you to draw irregular lines. Using the Freehand tool, lines can be drawn in different colours: black, red, white, etc; some drawing programs allow you to select from up to 16 million colours. Irregular lines can be drawn in any place within the drawing program screen.

If you want to correct mistakes or make changes, there are two ways of doing it. You can use the *Eraser* tool to rub out a small error, or you can start a new drawing by using the 'New' command in the File menu.

There are other drawing tools available. You should now try to use the tools that allow you to draw straight lines, squares or rectangles, circles and ellipses.

*Different drawing programs use different icons for the tools. Here are two types of symbol which are common.*

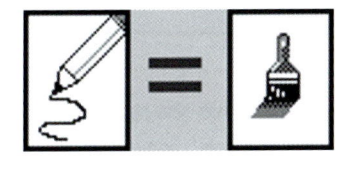

Freehand tool symbols

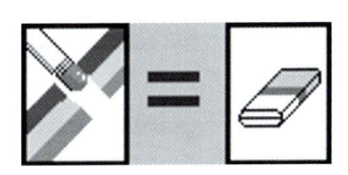

Eraser tool symbols

Unit K: Graphics

> Continue with the computer

**PRACTICE 1** Copy this drawing using the computer. If you make a mistake and want to start again, choose 'New' from the File menu. Or you can use the eraser tool.

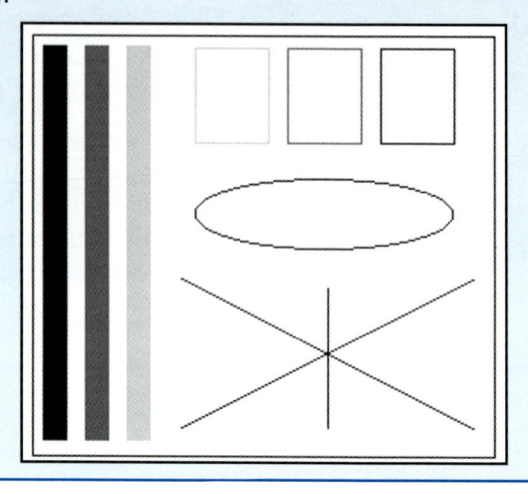

**PRACTICE 2** Copy this drawing on the computer using colour. If you make a mistake and want to start again, choose 'New' from the File menu. Or you can use the eraser tool.

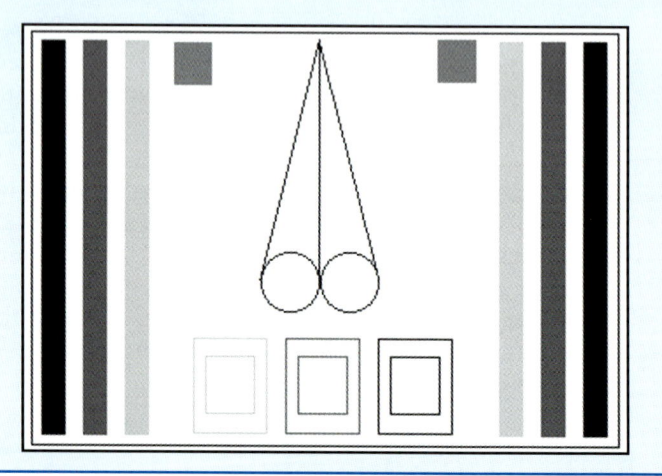

> Continue with the computer

# Unit K: Graphics

## ADVANTAGES OF GRAPHICS PROGRAMS

Rather than using pencil and paper, drawing and designing graphics on a computer has many important advantages. Here are a few:

- Changes can be made to a drawing on the screen very easily, very quickly and as substantially or as minimally as is needed.
- Different colours can be used very easily.
- There is a selection of different tools to draw curved lines, straight lines, rectangles and circles.
- If a paper copy of the graphic or drawing is needed, this can be delayed until it is complete.
- Graphics and drawings can be saved on disk: for example onto a floppy disk or hard disk. Changes can then be made at a later date.
- There is no need to keep paper copies of drawings. For companies that produce thousands of drawings, this can save a lot of space.
- The drawing can be extremely accurate. Since drawing programs allow you to zoom in and enlarge the drawing, an accuracy of 1/10 millimetre is easily obtained. Some programs work to an accuracy of 1/1000 of a millimetre!
- Graphics created on a computer can be copied into word-processed documents. When you print the document, the graphic is printed in the correct place.

There are many other advantages, as you will find out later.

### Keeping graphics

Once a drawing or graphic has been created it can be saved in the same way as any other file on the computer. Using the File menu and the 'Save As' option, your drawing can be kept in one of the many graphics file formats. At this stage of your skill development it is probably best to use the file format automatically proposed by the drawing program you are using (this occurs when you save the graphic).

Once a graphic has been saved as a file, it can be opened in a drawing program to enable it to be worked on again, or to be inserted into a word-processed or desktop publishing document. This is done using the Insert menu and choosing 'Picture' and then 'From File'.

---

Continue with the computer

## The uses of CAD and CAM in manufacturing

The use of CAD in the design of an item can make its manufacture much easier. Manufacturing machines connected to the CAD computer can 'read' the design information. They can then produce the item with little or no help from humans. For example, if, using CAD, you made a technical drawing of a screw, a machine such as a lathe could 'read' the drawing and automatically manufacture the screw for you. Similarly, if you designed an electronic circuit on a computer, assembly machines could automatically place the parts into precise position onto the circuit board.

## The fashion industry

Fashion designers still do most of their 'artistic work' using pencil and paper. Once the 'artistic' design is finished, they use CAD to make the pattern and plan the best way to cut it out of the smallest piece of material.

The factory will use the CAD data in their CAM cutting machines. The operators load the machines with whichever material is to be used. They can then stand back while the CAM machine does the work at very high speed.

*A 'fashion sketch'*

## A kitchen designer

Many kitchen designers use a CAD system to design a plan for a kitchen. The designer has a library of cupboards, ovens, ventilation hoods, and so on. The designer simply chooses a library item and places it down in the plan. Using CAD means that the plan can be designed quickly and easily.

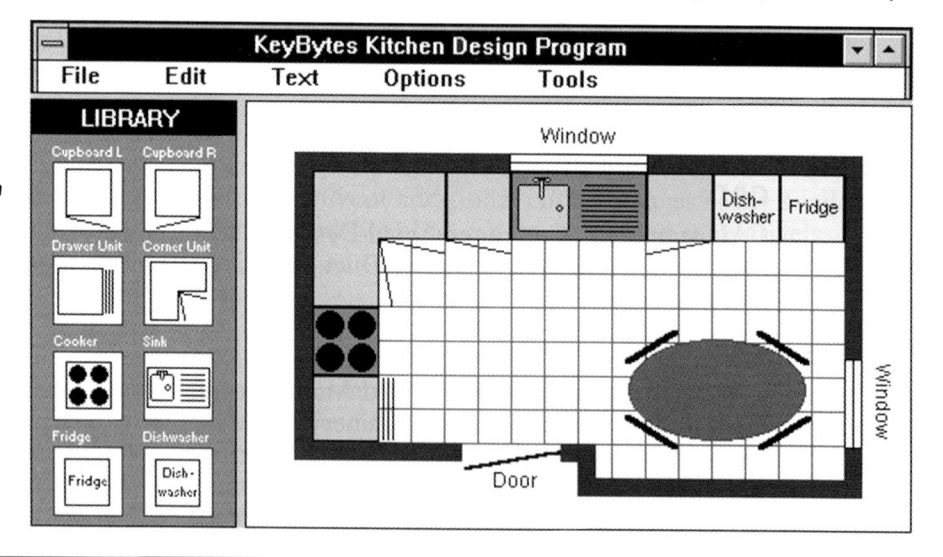

*The kitchen planner's library of drawings are shown in the left side of the window.*

The CAD program will show a 3D (three dimensional) picture of the kitchen. This lets the customer 'see' the kitchen before it's built. Often the 3D picture shows up mistakes that had not been seen earlier.

*CAD machines can show realistic 3D (three dimensional) pictures once a drawing is complete.*

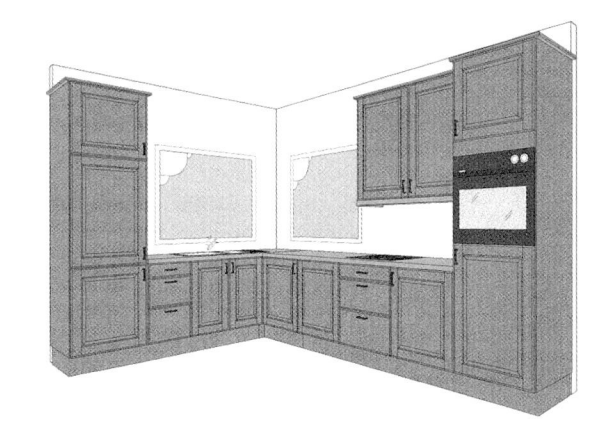

## Car designers

The CAD systems used by car designers have all the drawing tools you have used, but also many more. Their drawing program will let them:

- Choose any part of a drawing, then move it, or stretch it or turn it round.
- Zoom in to draw really small items, and zoom out to the whole shape.
- Draw and view things in three dimensions (3D).
- Copy a part of a drawing, then paste it into the same or another drawing.
- Draw 'in layers'. This can be very useful when they need to draw complicated things.
- Draw everything on a grid. A grid is a series of points spaced evenly all over the drawing area. Whatever is drawn starts and ends at the nearest grid point. One advantage of this is that you can join up lines very easily and accurately.

Almost every piece of a car is made by Computer-Aided Manufacture. All the machine instructions are taken from the CAD and CAM program.

## The uses of CAD and CAM in education

For schools there are packages that are designed to work with specific machinery in order to provide access to the whole process of designing and making with computers. Some machinery, such as sewing-machines, is now available with programming facilities. These facilities allow designs for embroidery to be programmed by pupils.

Unit K: *Graphics*

Although CAD and CAM are often associated with technology, other curriculum areas may also benefit. For example, the use of computer-aided design to explore the building of pyramids may allow pupils to develop a greater understanding of how technology and history are connected.

---

**Continue with the computer**

---

| PRACTICE 4 | Copy this drawing using the computer. If you make a mistake and want to start again, choose 'New' from the File menu. Or you can use the eraser tool. |

## SUMMARY SUMMARY SUMMARY SUMMARY SUMMARY

- The word 'graphic' means a picture. Usually it has been created on a computer – or has been scanned into a computer.

- Graphics can be created in a drawing program easily, quickly and accurately.

- Finished graphics can be saved onto a disk. As many copies as are needed can be printed. Graphics can be altered again later if more change is needed.

- Different drawing tools can be used to speed up the drawing work. The basic tools include freehand, eraser, circles, rectangles, lines, colours and special effects like spray paint.

Unit K: *Graphics*

## SUMMARY

- Hundreds of graphics can be contained on a single CD-ROM. These drawing libraries are sometimes called 'clipart'. Each drawing can be changed as needed and then copied into word-processed documents.

- Specialised drawing libraries are created by many firms. They use them to make drawings containing their own equipment faster and more accurate.

- CAD is short for Computer-Aided Design. It is used to help design things more easily, quickly and accurately. It is also used to give design data to CAM programs.

- CAM is short for Computer-Aided Manufacturing. CAD information can be used by CAM machines to manufacture things automatically.

- CAD/CAM is designing and manufacturing with computers.

---

**Continue with the computer**

---

**TASKS**

1. How could the simple use of graphics help students in your classroom?

   What advantages would there be for students with particular or special needs?

2. Consider some precise uses of clipart that would enhance a particular topic or unit of work.

   Find out whether the artwork you need is already available in school.

3. Consider the ways in which being able to design a physical environment may enhance or extend work in a particular area of your work.

   Find out what design packages are available in your school. The ICT co-ordinator should be able to assist you in this.

# Unit L

# Publishing Your Work

## INTRODUCTION

Computers are now commonly used for preparing documents ready for publication: that is to produce attractive and interesting page design ready for reproduction on paper or on screen. The purpose of good page design is to ensure the clarity of written text. The range of skills involved includes the writing and editing of text, arrangement of text and graphical images on the page, and printing or publishing on screen.

### Objectives

This chapter extends the work undertaken in Unit H. Further word processing skills are developed and some desktop publishing skills are introduced and practised.

By the end of this chapter you should be able to:

- Use a desktop publishing package to create a document with a professional look.

### Desktop publishing – or DTP

DTP is the abbreviation used for 'desktop publishing'.

The first DTP program went on sale in 1985. Its name was *Pagemaker*.

Now most word processing programs can do everything that the first *Pagemaker* program did – so special DTP programs aren't always needed.

However, newer types of multimedia DTP programs do more – they make it easy to create Internet pages and on-screen presentations that include video and other moving pictures.

### Desktop publishing – its nature and purpose

Publishing has until recently involved a series of separate processes: writing, editing, designing, picture creation, typesetting, scanning, page layout, checking and printing. All of these processes can in theory now be carried out by a single person using a desktop publishing package. Using a computer to publish work may be quicker, more accurate and may result in a more attractive product.

However it is worth remembering that the computer itself has no aesthetic skills, and that it is possible to create published material that is confusing to look at and hard to understand. Some simple guidelines are included in this unit to help prevent this.

Multimedia DTP work needs a wide variety of additional skills in:

- Design
- Writing and word processing
- Graphics
- Sound and video

This unit will help you to create interesting documents which can be printed out or published on the computer screen.

*A few different types of 'desktop publishing' program. DTP is the abbreviation most people call them by.*

**Key words**

| | | |
|---|---|---|
| | Desktop publishing | The process of using a computer to position text and graphics onto a page during the design of a document. |
| | Frame | A 'box' in which text and pictures can be placed in a desktop publishing document. |
| | Import | Moving text, graphics or other data into a desktop publishing page straight from a word processing or other program. |

| | |
|---|---|
| **Intranet** | An intranet is a big 'library' of data that everyone on a computer network can use.<br>Find out about intranets in Unit O. |
| **Multimedia** | A mixture of different types of computer output. For example, text, music and video all mixed together in one on-screen document. |
| **On-screen** | Documents that you create need not be printed. They can be shown on a single computer screen, or on all the screens in your school or college, or millions of screens if it is published on the Internet. |
| **Template** | The design arrangement of frames that will appear on each desktop publishing page. |

---

Continue with the computer

---

## WHO DO YOU WANT TO READ IT?

### Design for a purpose

The first thing to consider is the audience for your prospective publication. The audience for the work may be parents, students, or other teachers, all of whom will require a different approach. This consideration of the purpose of the publication affects not only the writing style, but choice of page layout, typestyle, inclusion of pictures, graphs and tables, and last but not least, the colours used.

### Small children ...

Books for small children should use typestyles that are easy to read. The typesize should be large with only a few words on each page.

### Young teenagers ...

Younger teenagers may prefer a very different type of design. They like things 'zappy', unstructured and very colourful.

Most books or magazines for young teenagers use a range of different typestyles in different sizes. The text is written in short paragraphs with many pictures, big headings and bold labels and captions.

Unit L: Publishing Your Work

## WHITE'S ALLRIGHT

"I've got red hair and very pale skin. Every summer my mates take the mick and call me 'milkbottle'. The problem is I don't tan, I burn!"
**Terri, 13, London**

**Marchu says**: "There's a simple answer – fake it! There are great fake tans on the market, so get practising. Or turn your paleness to your advantage. Explain that celebs like Madonna keep out of the sun cos it's damaging. If they keep taking the mick, are they really the friends you want to have around?"

## FLYING HIGH

"I'm going on holiday with my parents for the first time but I'm terrified of flying. What can I do?"
**Jane, 12, Salisbury**

**Anthony says:** "You are more likely to die in a car than in a plane – flying is one of the safest ways to travel. But if you're really worried, talk to your parents. Maybe your doctor can give you something to calm you down, or your local airport might run a course for your fears (try the Yellow Pages). Good luck!"

*The design, the words and the graphics in this magazine are clearly aimed at young teenagers.*

### Newspapers ...

Newspaper companies undertake research to find out what different groups of people want from their publication. They decide on a target audience and design the newspaper to be attractive to that target audience.

The target audience for some newspapers is people who want short news reports plus lots of fun stories and news about 'showbusiness' and entertainment.

Unit L: Publishing Your Work

The page size of these newspapers is relatively small: they are 'tabloid' in size – hence the generic name given to them.

Tabloid newspapers use big, bold headlines which are often designed to be amusing. These newspapers report stories based on the activities of TV and film actors. They have pictures, cartoons and 'snippets' of information, as well as short reports about important news.

## R WHAT A SHAME

*Vauxhall Wreck-tra ... the R-reg car that George smashed up*

By JAMIE PYATT

RED-faced delivery driver George Hendry yesterday became the first man in Britain to crash an R-reg car — just TWO HOURS after they were launched.

George, 59, smashed up a £14,000 Vauxhall Vectra after hitting a lorry when he was dazzled by headlights.

Grandad George picked up the car in Southampton, Hants, at the stroke of midnight and began driving to Scotland to deliver it to owner Danny McCallum.

He had clocked up less than 100 miles when he crashed on the

### George KOs motor after two hours

M40 near Banbury, Oxfordshire. George said: "I feel terrible — it's very embarrassing. I hope the owner forgives me." Vauxhall are to replace the car.

Danny, 35, said: "I'm gutted. You couldn't print what I want to say about the delivery driver."

A Sun *report*

Other newspapers have a target audience who like to know lots about the political and financial news from around the world. These newspapers are written in a more serious way.

The text reports are longer and give more detail. The headlines are smaller and not so jokey. Usually these 'serious' newspapers have a page size that is twice as big as the smaller papers: they are 'broadsheet' size.

## Compare the difference

Look at the different way the *Sun* (a tabloid) and the *Daily Telegraph* (a broadsheet) reported the same car crash.

The *Sun* uses two jokey headlines, a picture and just a short text report. The *Daily Telegraph* gives much more information – but it's all quite serious, and not much fun!

### First R-reg crash inside four hours

**By Paul Marston, Transport Correspondent**

ONE of the first R-registered cars was written off within four hours of leaving the showroom yesterday.

The £14,000 Vauxhall Vectra Arctic crashed on the M40 near Banbury, Oxon, on its way from a Hampshire dealership to an eager customer in Dundee.

It suffered "very extensive" damage in a collision with the M40's central reservation barrier and is thought to be beyond repair. The delivery driver was unhurt.

Brian Batchelor, the dealership's managing director, said he was shocked at first but "began to see the funny side of it". Vauxhall said the buyer would receive a new car "within a few days".

The owner, Danny McCallum, 35, a salesman, said: "I only found out when I phoned my boss. I didn't believe him and thought he was winding me up.

"By coincidence, my car didn't start this morning for the first time in two years and I had to push-start it.

"It'll be another month or so now before I get a replacement. It was a limited edition and they haven't got any more left."

The incident occurred at 3.40am yesterday, more than two hours after the AA had received its first emergency call from an R-reg driver, whose car had come to a halt with a faulty clutch on the M3 in Hampshire.

In Wetherby, North Yorks, a 64-year-old driver pranged his £37,000 R-reg Mercedes 320 just seconds after leaving the showroom at 9 am. He pulled out of a junction and crashed into a Jaguar.

By last night the motoring organisations had dealt with more than 50 R-reg call-outs, with the most common problem being drivers who could not understand their new car's electrical gadgetry.

More than a dozen locked themselves out of their cars or could not start the engine because they had not turned off the immobiliser.

By Monday the AA expects to have received 500 calls from new owners. "The problem is that so many cars are going off the forecourt in the first few days that dealers do not have time to familiarise customers with the details of how they work."

Manufacturers expect to sell 500,000 new cars this month, a quarter of the annual total. This year's may be the last August rush, as regulations due to be finalised shortly are likely to lead to registration plates being changed every six months instead of every 12.

*The same story is treated differently in the* Daily Telegraph.

---

**Continue with the computer**

---

## DESIGNING THE DOCUMENT

Good design is very important in every type of document.

Publications can be designed to be of particular interest to their intended audience. Good design ensures that the reader understands the message of the text without undue effort.

The sort of documents you may need to 'publish', and consider using a desktop publishing package for are:

- information for parents
- school prospectus
- reports

- worksheets
- information for other staff, etc.

Here are some guidelines which, if followed, help to ensure clarity.

- Avoid including too much information on one page.
- White space is important. The margins ensure that the document does not appear too daunting.
- Space can be used to draw attention to a particular part of the page.
- People tend to look at pictures before headlines. Arrange pictures, headlines and text so that they complement each other.
- Too many changes of font and type size appear visually chaotic. You may want this effect, but if not, use one font and logical changes of size.
- Bold and italic type are more effective for highlighting important text than underlining. Underlining gives text a slightly 'dated' look.
- Fonts with serifs are regarded as slightly more formal in their 'tone'.
- Look at the design of publications you are given to read, and decide which of their features you find effective. You can then incorporate these into your own designs where they are appropriate.

### Text fonts

Some typefaces (fonts) are good for text, others are good for headings. There is a very big range to choose from. The differences between one font and another can be quite small but that difference can be important to the reader.

**glad**   This font is good for small children who learn to write using this shape for the letter a and g.

**glad**   This font has 'serifs' (small feet on all the letters). It's good for text, but not so good for headings.

**glad**   This is a 'sans serif' font (without 'feet'). Sans serif fonts are often used in informal reports, or in headings.

*glad*   This 'script' style of font is for invitations and perhaps certificates. It is not usually used for ordinary text.

## Font size

It's not too hard to read small characters if the line of text is short. Look at a telephone directory – the words are easy to read even though the text is small.

| | |
|---|---|
| **Fussy D**, St James' Park | (0213) 345441 |
| **Fyfe F**, Highfield Road | (0529) 352234 |
| **Gadd H**, 12 Elland Road | (0332) 112345 |
| **Gardener P**, 7 White Hart Lane | (0332) 145632 |
| **Georgiou M**, 83 Filbert Street | (0241) 345269 |
| **Giannasi V**, 7a Villa Park | (0235) 143452 |
| **Gibbons M**, 141 Riverside | (0231) 252041 |
| **Gilchrist C**, 5 Anfield Road | (0332) 157221 |
| **Gillard K**, 42 Old Trafford Street | (0331) 578139 |
| **Ginder V**, 6 Stamford Bridge | (0123) 535123 |

Bigger text sizes are needed in longer lines. Also use bigger text sizes when you expect readers to find the document difficult to read.

Extremely big text sizes are used when the text is for people to read as they walk by (like posters). Or when it is required to catch attention, like newspaper and magazine headings.

## Graphics and space!

To make documents attract readers, choose a small number of high quality *graphics*.

Work out the best arrangement for mixing the text with the pictures.

Don't try to put too much on a page. *Blank space* is important. It makes the text stand out and easier to read.

Choose the best font, in the best size and with plenty of space around the text and graphics and there's a good chance your words will be read.

*Careful choice of how to mix the text with the graphics can make the publication interesting.*

Unit L: *Publishing Your Work*

# ← is your diet dodgy?

## "You can eat a lot and still be healthy"

Charlotte, 16, from London, works as an office administrator and part-time model. She's 5ft 8ins and weighs 10 and a half stone.

**Breakfast:**
"Two slices of toast with margarine and a grapefruit. A glass of orange juice."

**Morning Snacks:**
"Apple and a banana. Cup of tea and a glass of water."

**Lunch:**
"Tuna and pasta salad and two slices of bread. Drinks of lemonade and sparkling water."

**Afternoon Snacks:**
"A few biscuits and a cup of tea."

**Dinner:**
"Chicken and pasta with a salad. Water and lemonade to drink."

**Evening Snacks:**
"Packet of jelly babies and lots of water to take to bed!"

**Exercise:**
"I spend about two hours at the gym every Sunday and about an hour-and-a-half on Tuesday and Thursday evenings. I also do an aerobics class on Monday and Wednesday evenings."

### Charlotte's verdict:

**"I can't stand junk food"**
"I like to have a least three pieces of fruit a day, especially bananas because they give you energy. My favourite meal is pasta, and I also eat a lot of bread and potatoes. I do eat sweets, biscuits and crisps whenever I get cravings and I drink loads of water. I think you can eat a lot and still be healthy. My friends always say, 'Where do you put it all?' Basically, I eat when I want to and as much as I want to, but I think I eat healthily."

### Dr Moira's comments:

**"Now, this is healthy!"**
"Charlotte's diet is very reasonable. A person should have five portions of fruit or vegetables a day and Charlotte is doing pretty well on that front. Orange juice at breakfast is very good because it increases your absorption of iron. What she could do is sometimes have breakfast cereal with milk to increase her intake of calcium from the milk, and iron from the cereal. She could sometimes eat wholemeal bread for fibre instead of white.
"She could have yoghurt, again for calcium because she's not taking much

---

This page is from a magazine aimed at teenage girls. Notice the design:

- The big picture immediately catches the eye.
- The main heading is interesting and it uses large, bold typestyles which lead gradually into the main text.
- The main text is quite short so it can be read quickly.
- The writing style is lighthearted throughout.
- The whole page looks interesting and 'inviting'.
- Although you can't see them here the colours used are attractive and help maintain interest in the page.

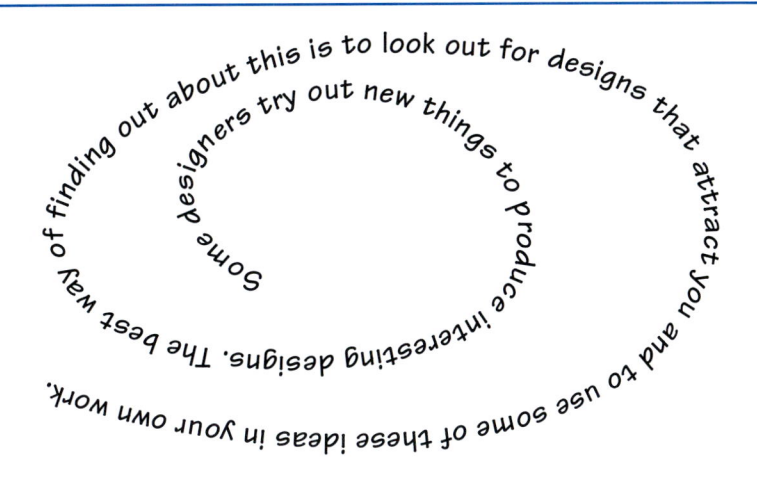

Some of the way of finding out about this is to look out for designs that attract you and to use some of these ideas in your own work. The best way designers try out new things to produce interesting designs.

*Continue with the computer*

## FRAMES AND TEMPLATES

In DTP programs, text and graphics are typed into *frames*.

A frame is a 'box' that holds the text or graphics. Frames can be made visible or invisible on the screen, as you choose.

An advantage of using frames is that you can easily move everything in the frame to a new position on the page. Or the whole frame can be cut, and pasted onto a different page.

Before starting to type, create a series of frames that will give the design which suits your purpose. This will become the *template* for the publication. The arrangement of each page will be the same as the template design.

The template may be two columns with a headline at the top, as in the diagram over the page.

Perhaps a single column with wide margins around the text would suit your document better.

It may be that something more complicated is required: perhaps five columns with a box in the middle of the page for a picture.

When you are satisfied with a template you can *save* it for reuse.

# Unit L: Publishing Your Work

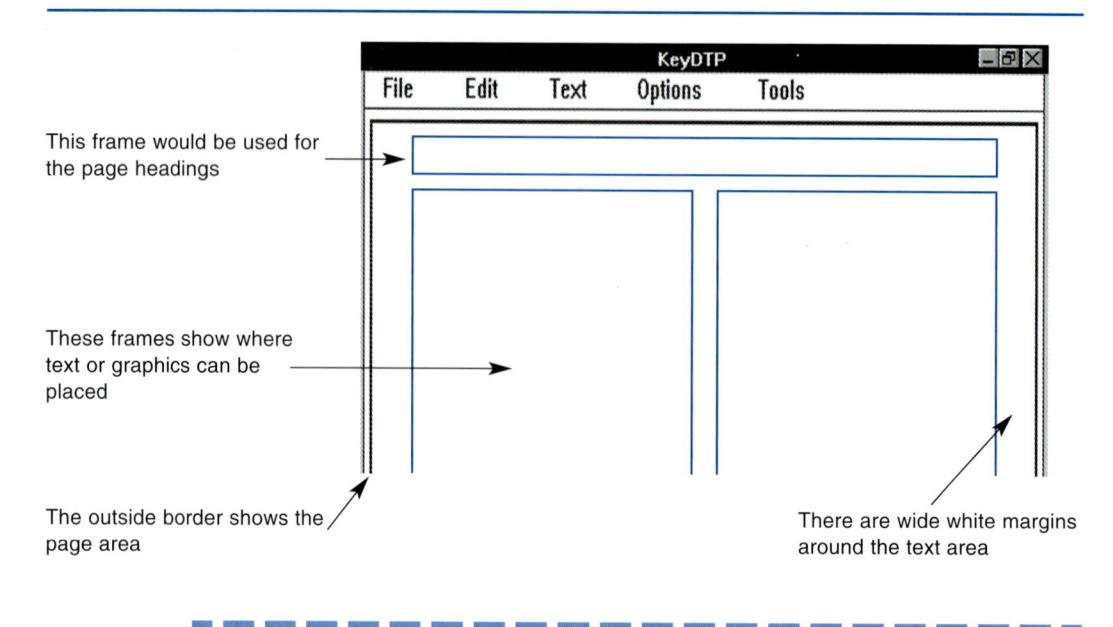

This frame would be used for the page headings

These frames show where text or graphics can be placed

The outside border shows the page area

There are wide white margins around the text area

---

**Continue with the computer**

---

## USING DTP

Any word-processed document file can be copied (*imported*) into the DTP program. Or the document can be typed straight into the DTP program.

Simple drawings can be made using the DTP program – or they too can be imported from a graphics program.

Photographs can be scanned and imported. So can graphs, tables and spreadsheet calculations.

---

**Continue with the computer**

---

## HYPERLINKS

Many documents are never printed onto paper. Instead they are published to be read *on screen*. The problem with this is that only one page can be seen at a time. It is not easy to 'flick through' pages like it is in a book. A solution is to insert hyperlinks into the document.

Hyperlinks let you jump from page to page in an on-screen document.

Unit L: Publishing Your Work

*Create a hyperlink to jump from page to page, or file to file. Text, sound, graphics or video can all be hyperlinked to each other.*

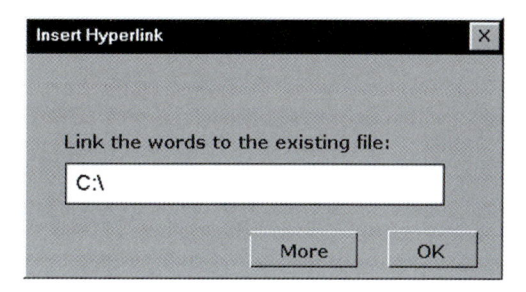

It's a good idea to make a list of headings at the start of any long document. If these are done as hyperlinks then, by clicking on the heading you want, you'll be taken immediately to that section of the on-screen document.

**Multimedia hyperlinks**

Hyperlinks can be used in other ways – they help you create *multimedia documents*. A hyperlink to a sound file will play sound. A hyperlink to a video file will show the video. A hyperlink to any other text or graphic file will display the contents of the file on the screen.

Hyperlinks are very important in the design of Internet and intranet pages (you'll learn more about these in Unit O). When you are using DTP to design on-screen documents think about the links that can be made to other files and documents. This is a straightforward way to improve the usefulness of your documents.

Words that are hyperlinked appear on the screen often (but not always) coloured blue and underlined.

*Graphics* can also be hyperlinked to other files and documents. Click on any hyperlinked graphic and the new file or document will come onto the screen.

```
Continue with the computer
```

## SUMMARY  SUMMARY  SUMMARY  SUMMARY  SUMMARY

- DTP is the abbreviation for desktop publishing.

- Designing and producing a publication uses the skills of writing, editing, designing, picture creation, typesetting, page layout, scanning.

- Desktop publishing programs can make the design and production of publications easier and quicker.

## Unit L: *Publishing Your Work*

**SUMMARY**

- Desktop publishing documents can be printed onto paper or published 'on screen'.
- Desktop publishing allows you to experiment with different typefaces and different designs on the computer screen.
- Before you start to design, it is important to consider the audience for the work.
- Documents and publications must be written and designed to be attractive to their intended audience.
- White space is important: it can be used to direct attention to particular parts of a page.
- Position the main headline, pictures and text to attract the reader's attention.
- Text and pictures are placed into frames on the desktop publishing screen.
- Create and arrange into frames to suit the page design you want to make. This design then becomes the template for all pages.
- You can import text and pictures into the desktop publishing document from other programs.
- The differences between word-processing programs and desktop publishing programs are diminishing.
- By using hyperlinks in a DTP document it is possible to jump to another page, or to another file – including sound and video.
- Hyperlink words are often shown on the screen in blue, and are underlined. Graphics can have hyperlinks too. Most Internet and intranet pages use hyperlinks.

**TASKS**

1. Find out if your school has a desktop publishing package which is available for you to use.
2. Use DTP to produce a document for parents or students.
3. Consider how students might use DTP in their work. How can DTP packages enhance their learning experiences?

# Unit M

# Computers Doing the Work

## INTRODUCTION

The progress of technology has led to great changes in the working lives of most people. In the past, most jobs were done by hand. Now machines do a great deal of our work *automatically*. Many machines have become 'computerised' over the last 50 years, that is they are controlled by computer programs. This unit looks at how computer-controlled machines have taken over some types of work.

## Objectives

In this unit you will:

- learn how to give robots instructions to control the way they work.
- consider some of the uses for robots and how they may be used in the future.
- use a program to control a cartoon robotic machine.

A robotic arm at work in a car factory.

Unit M: *Computers Doing the Work*

**Key words**

| | | |
|---|---|---|
| | Computer-controlled machine | Any machine that has a computer controlling what it does or when it does it. The 'computer' can be just a few small silicon chips, or more like your desktop computer. |
| | Robotics | The use of computer-controlled machines that do work people find difficult. This might be because the work is heavy, dangerous, tiring, needs to be done in a small spaces, etc. |
| | Sensor | Sensors measure things like sound, heat, and light. They are the 'eyes and ears' of computer-controlled robotic machines. |

```
Continue with the computer
```

## COMPUTER-CONTROLLED MACHINES AND ROBOTS

### In the factory

You can find computer-controlled machines in the home, in cars, in offices and in factories. We have already seen how computers and digital processors help to control equipment we use at home and at work. Machinery that carries out mechanical tasks and is controlled by a computer is often called *robotic*. At one time people thought of a robot as something like a mechanical human, but now we use the term to refer to a wide range of machinery.

Robots are computer-controlled machines that often carry out dirty, difficult, dangerous or heavy tasks in factories. They can perform a task repeatedly and without rest. For this reason, they are used extensively on assembly lines, where the same task must be completed on thousands of identical items. The automobile industry, for example, has developed robotic applications for most of its production processes.

### On the farm

Robots and other computer-controlled machines are not only found in factories; they play an important role in farming. Some dairy farmers use robots to milk cows. When the cow arrives in the milking shed, the robot gives it some fodder, which calms it down. The robot then uses sensors to feel where the cow's udders are and the cow is milked automatically. Since the cow can be milked more often, it produces more milk.

On farms with a fodder machine, every cow has a collar containing a small radio transmitter. This allows the fodder machine to detect which cow is at the feeding trough. The machine records exactly how much that cow has had to eat already that day and how much it is allowed. In this way, every cow gets exactly the right amount to eat.

Using information from the milking robot, a computer can automatically record how much milk each cow produces. This is called *data logging*. The data can be used to decide if a cow is giving too little milk. If it is, the farmer has to decide why.

*A cow can be fed, milked and weighed by machine.*

```
Continue with the computer
```

## GIVING INSTRUCTIONS TO MACHINES

All computer-controlled machines need instructions to control how they work and these instructions are called a *program*.

Someone who creates a program is called a programmer. If you have set the alarm on a digital watch, or set up a video recorder, or set the washing machine to do a wash, then you have already done some simple programming.

Other programs are much more difficult to create. For example, all of the software you use on the computer, such as word processors, games and *KeyBytes*, are programs. These use instructions written in a code or language recognised by the computer. Complex computer languages convert logical instructions into machine codes. (In Unit D, we looked at one such code – the binary code.)

Unit M: *Computers Doing the Work*

The language you have learnt for Robby the Robot is simple: 'l' means left, 'r' means right, and so on. Other programming languages, such as Visual Basic, Pascal, C and C++, are much more complex, but allow you to do much more.

```
Call Writeslowly(500, 500, Black, Grey, "How does a robot
know what to do?", "", 1)

Call Writeslowly(500, 1000, Black, Grey, "Well, you have to
give it instructions.", "instructions", 1)

Call Writeslowly(500, 1500, Black, Grey, "Most robots are
stupid.", "stupid", 1)

Call Picture(500, 2000, "M_DURR.BMP", 2)
```

*This is a small part of the KeyBytes program written in Visual Basic. The complete program contains about 50,000 lines of instruction!*

- - - - - - - - - - - - - - - - - - - - - - - - - - - - - -
                     Continue with the computer
- - - - - - - - - - - - - - - - - - - - - - - - - - - - - -

## PROGRAMS – CORRECT INSTRUCTIONS IN THE RIGHT ORDER

Computer-controlled machines can help you do some tasks more effectively. Let's take a simple example from everyday life. Most cameras, even inexpensive ones, contain a computer that can set the camera to the appropriate settings. It senses what type of film you are using, measures the amount of light, decides whether the flash is needed, sets the correct exposure time, measures the distance and sets the correct focus. It does everything except take the picture!

- **Functions**
- Power zoom with auto focus
- Auto, Fill-in, Off flash
- Red-eye reduction (Pre-flash)
- Fuzzy zoom (Intelligent exposure)
- Portrait zoom (Intelligent framing)
- Step zoom
- Continuous shooting
- Interval shooting
- Multi-exposure shooting
- Remote control
- Date imprinting

Unit M: Computers Doing the Work

## Flow charts

One way to get things in the right order is to draw a flow chart. This is one for the camera program.

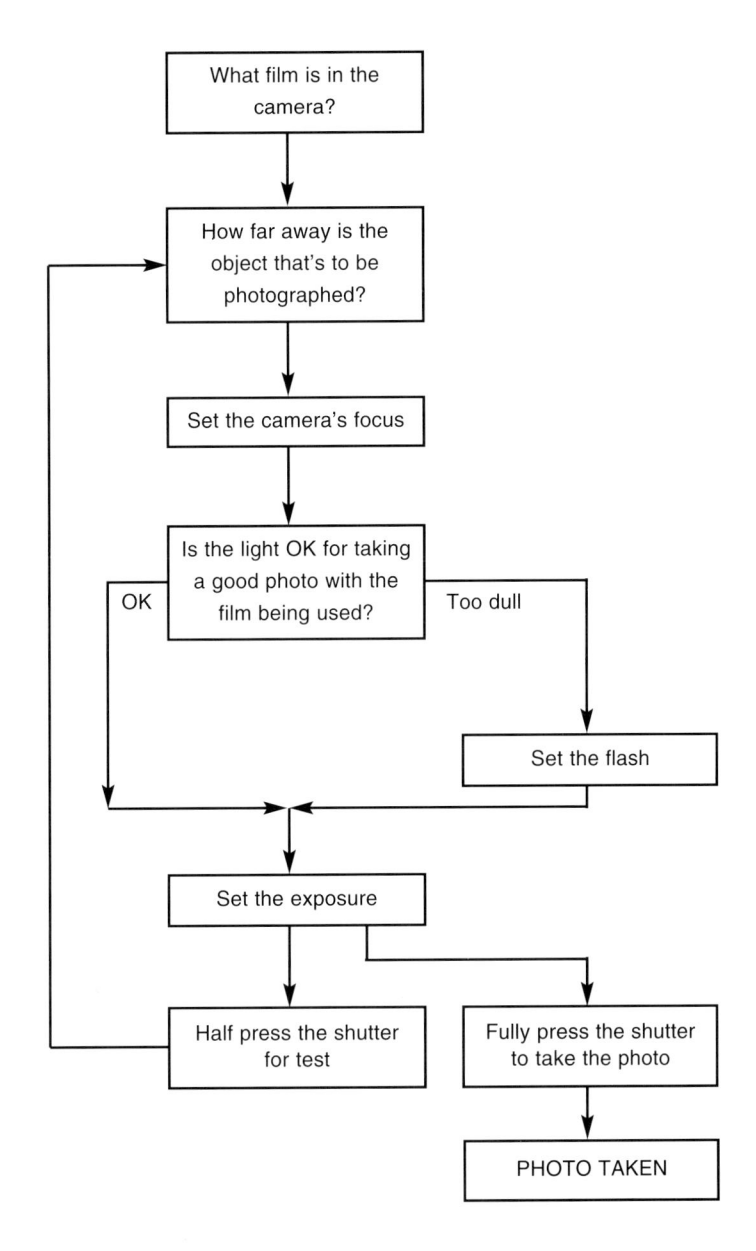

```
What film is in the camera?
        ↓
How far away is the object that's to be photographed?
        ↓
Set the camera's focus
        ↓
Is the light OK for taking a good photo with the film being used?
   OK ↓        Too dull →  Set the flash
        ↓                      ↓
Set the exposure ←─────────────┘
        ↓
Half press the shutter for test    Fully press the shutter to take the photo
                                            ↓
                                      PHOTO TAKEN
```

## Changing the program

Some computer-controlled robots can be re-programmed to change the task they do. For example, a car factory can re-program a paint-sprayer robot to paint a different size or shape of car. This means that the same machine can be used for more than one job. Machines controlled by computers are normally very quick, accurate and seldom break down.

Unit M: *Computers Doing the Work*

Computer-controlled machines usually need fewer workers than machines controlled by hand. This saves money on wages, which are often the greatest cost to a factory. There are some factories where few people can be seen. Computers, machines and robots have taken over much of the work.

Computers can do a great deal, but most cannot react to a situation that has not been allowed for in their program. They just carry on and do exactly what they are told. If a paint-sprayer robot is presented with an already painted car, it doesn't stop and think, 'Humm, that's odd, it's already painted.' It would just carry on and paint it again. Humans, on the other hand, may be slower and perhaps less reliable, but at least they are intelligent and can change what they do very quickly.

However, there are now machines with *feedback* systems that use information to allow the robot to 'intelligently' respond to changes. At its simplest, this may mean gathering data from a tag on a cow to know whether the cow has just been milked. More complex machines use sensors to gather information about the environment, responding to changes in temperature and humidity to control environmental systems.

```
Continue with the computer
```

## MORE EFFECTIVE CONTROL

Even the simple program language we used for Robby can be made easier and quicker to write. We did this by writing r4 instead of rrrr.

The program that guides Robby through the passage gets information from the sensors. In Robby's case, the sensors detect the walls. The computer processes the information from the sensors, decides what to do and then controls what the robot does next.

We call this *measurement and control*. The program uses sensors to detect, or measure, something (in this case the walls). The program then controls what happens next. This process is shown in the following diagram.

Unit M: Computers Doing the Work

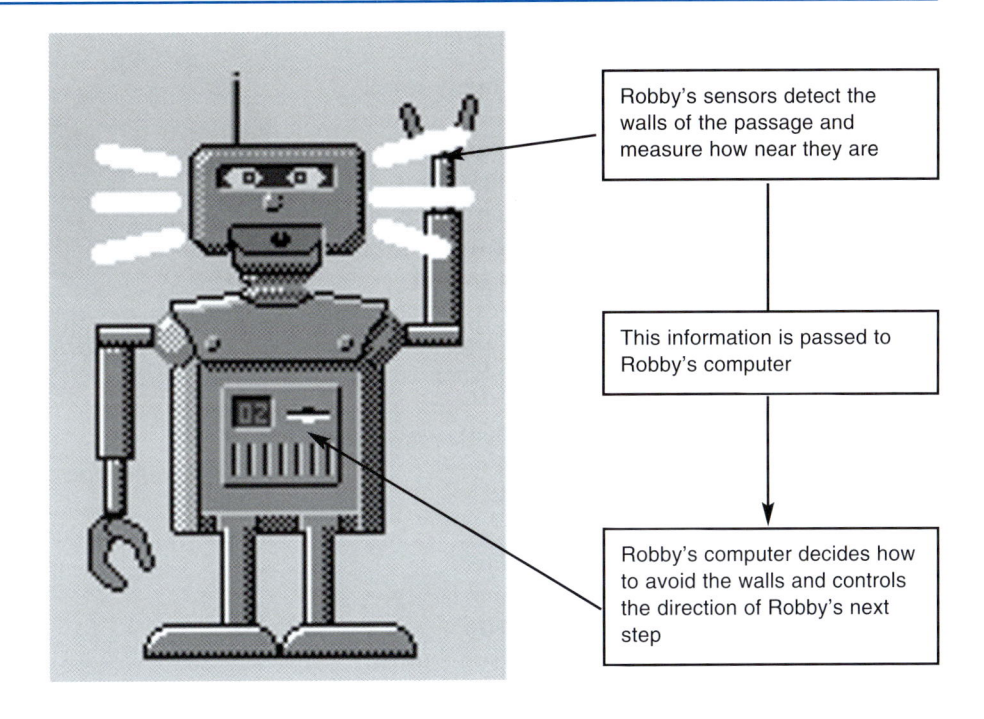

Robby's sensors detect the walls of the passage and measure how near they are

This information is passed to Robby's computer

Robby's computer decides how to avoid the walls and controls the direction of Robby's next step

```
Continue with the computer
```

## MEASUREMENT AND CONTROL

Examples of measurement and control are all around us. Let's look at a few.

### Greenhouses

The greenhouse example in the *KeyBytes* program shows how sensors are used to measure sunlight and a programmed computer is used to control the lights in the greenhouse. Many greenhouses also use computer-controlled equipment for automatically measuring and controlling the watering, feeding and heating of all the different crops.

*This device measures and controls the humidity within a greenhouse.*

127

### Car engines

Computers are used for many jobs in a car. For example, they measure the engine's temperature and performance. This information is used to control how much fuel is sent to the engine. This can make the engine perform with greater efficiency. The car uses less petrol and does less damage to the environment. Many cars have engine computers that perform more than 12 million calculations every second.

*An engine management computer.*

### Hospitals

Hospitals can use computer-controlled machines connected to alarms to measure a person's pulse and breathing. If the person's pulse or breathing is too fast or too slow, the alarm sounds and the nurses are alerted.

Heart pacemakers are small computer-controlled machines that can be fitted inside the body. The pacemaker contains a small computer which measures and controls the person's heartbeat.

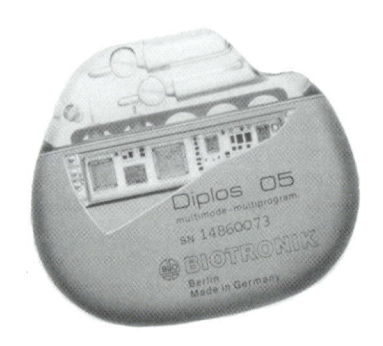

*A pacemaker*

### Burglar alarms

Burglar alarm systems use measurement and control. Sensors measure whether a person has entered or is about to enter a room. When a movement is detected by the sensor, it sends a signal to the computer, which sounds the alarm.

The most popular types of sensor for burglar alarms are door switches and infra-red detectors. Door switches are fitted somewhere around the edge of the door. When the door opens, the switch signals to the computer, which sounds the alarm. Infra-red detectors detect invisible infra-red light. All warm objects, even cold-hearted burglars, give out infra-red light. The detector constantly looks for any movement of infra-red light and sounds the alarm if any is detected.

```
Continue with the computer
```

## ROBOTS IN THE FUTURE

In the future, we are likely to see more and more examples of robots at work. An increasing range of tasks can be undertaken by robots, from simple cleaning operations to complex medical procedures.

Even now, experimental robots are used to assist with operations. For example, they can control the position of a camera deep inside the patient's body. The surgeon can move the camera automatically by turning his or her head while looking at the computer monitor. The robot uses sensors to detect the position of the surgeon's head, then moves the camera into the correct position. The robot replaces the job of the camera operator and allows the surgeon to concentrate on the operation.

Experimental robots have also been produced that copy the actions of a surgeon, who may be thousands of kilometres away in a different country.

Delicate sensors coupled with powerful programs now enable machines to respond to their environment and often they can react quickly without waiting for new instructions from the operator. For example, equipment used in exploring the depths of the ocean has been designed to protect itself from unexpected hazards.

Machines that can behave in this way are said to have 'artificial intelligence'.

*This robot, called Kismet, responds to visual stimuli.*

### Artificial intelligence under our roads!

Old sewage, water, gas and oil tunnels and pipelines must be inspected and repaired. Often they are too narrow or dangerous to be done by workmen.

Unit M: *Computers Doing the Work*

Our picture shows an 'inspection and repair' robot being slid into a narrow tunnel opening. Its sensors find a way through narrow winding tunnels and over small blockages. It can drill through bigger blockages or collect samples of fallen rocks etc. to bring back to the surface for proper inspection.

*Sending the pipeline 'inspection and repair' robot on its way!*

```
Continue with the computer
```

## SUMMARY SUMMARY SUMMARY SUMMARY SUMMARY

- Computer-controlled machines have changed the way people live and work. They have replaced many low-skilled jobs and created new jobs for people who have new skills.

- Computer-controlled machines can be tiny, like a digital watch, or very large, like a robotic welding arm in a car factory.

- Robotic computer-controlled machines are used in most factories, but also in hospitals, warehouses, and even farms.

- Unlike humans, robots can work without rest. They can do heavy work and can work in dangerous conditions.

- Robots and other computer-controlled machines need programming before they can work.

- A program is a set of computer instructions.

- The programs must be accurate and the instructions must be in the correct order.

## SUMMM

- Flow charts are a way of working out the order of the program.
- Some computer-controlled machines can be re-programmed to change the tasks they do.
- Sensors detect or measure things such as light, heat, infra-red light.
- The sensors send information back to the computer, which is programmed to control an activity.
- Measurement and control is where sensors measure changes and then the computer controls a response.

> Continue with the computer

### TASKS

1. Consider how an understanding of programming may help students to understand logical sequences.

   Is a knowledge of how robots are controlled transferable to other activities in your classroom, eg data logging or 'logo' activities?

2. How would you plan to include an understanding of the impact of technology on society in your classroom?

   In working with students in your school, you should consider some of the ethical questions raised by these developments.

3. Are measurement and control applications relevant to the lessons you teach? Check and amend your schemes of work to ensure appropriate coverage.

# Unit N
# Computers in Daily Life

## INTRODUCTION

Almost everyone in developed countries uses computers every day!

Computers are everywhere in our lives. If all the computers in the world broke down, our way of life would need to become very different.

## Objectives

This unit provides an overview of ways in which computers are used in everyday life.

**Key words**

| | |
|---|---|
| Security check | To make sure that the person trying to use a computer is the person allowed to do so. |
| | When a bank card is used the bank's computer makes a security check before money is given out. |
| Interactive whiteboard | A special whiteboard which is linked to a computer. The white screen is interactive because writing on it or touching it inputs data to the computer. |
| | The finished work can be saved onto the computer's disk. |

```
Continue with the computer
```

Unit N: *Computers in Daily Life*

## SMALL COMPUTERS IN BIG EQUIPMENT

A 'desktop' or 'laptop' computer system is needed to run *KeyBytes* and most of the other programs you use in the classroom. Desktop and laptop computers are designed to do many jobs and because of this they are relatively large. But most computers are designed to *do just one job* – and so the 'computer' part of the equipment can be tiny.

These tiny computers are usually deep inside the equipment they control. For example a video player has a computer inside it which controls when the video will record, when it will switch off, when it will change channel, when it will rewind the tape, etc.

A remote control is used to set the video. It *programs* the video's computer.

Pocket calculators, microwave cookers, central-heating controls, washing machines, burglar alarms are all examples of equipment controlled by their own small computer.

Most modern car engines are *monitored* and *controlled* by small computers. In fact the computers in an ordinary car are more powerful than in the Apollo spacecraft that made the first landing on the moon!

### Computers in traffic

Some lorries and private cars use a digital traffic and map system to choose the best route and avoid traffic jams. The system is kept up to date by roadside sensors and also by receiving digital signals from satellites floating high in the sky.

*A digital traffic and map system mounted on a car dashboard.*

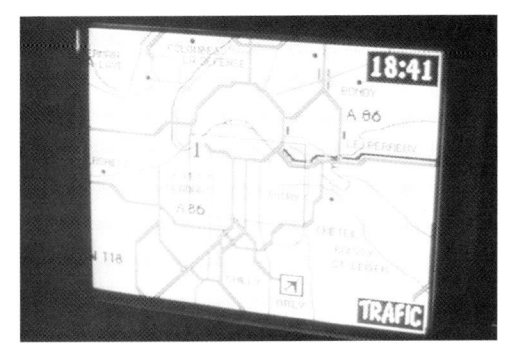

Traffic lights also use computers. They use sensors in the road or above the lights to make sure that vehicles wait the shortest possible time.

Every set of traffic lights needs to have a program which lets traffic move as smoothly as possible.

Look at the *flow chart* over the page. It shows how a program can test for something then 'loop' round and test again, and again, and again. It goes on like this until it reaches a time limit.

Unit N: *Computers in Daily Life*

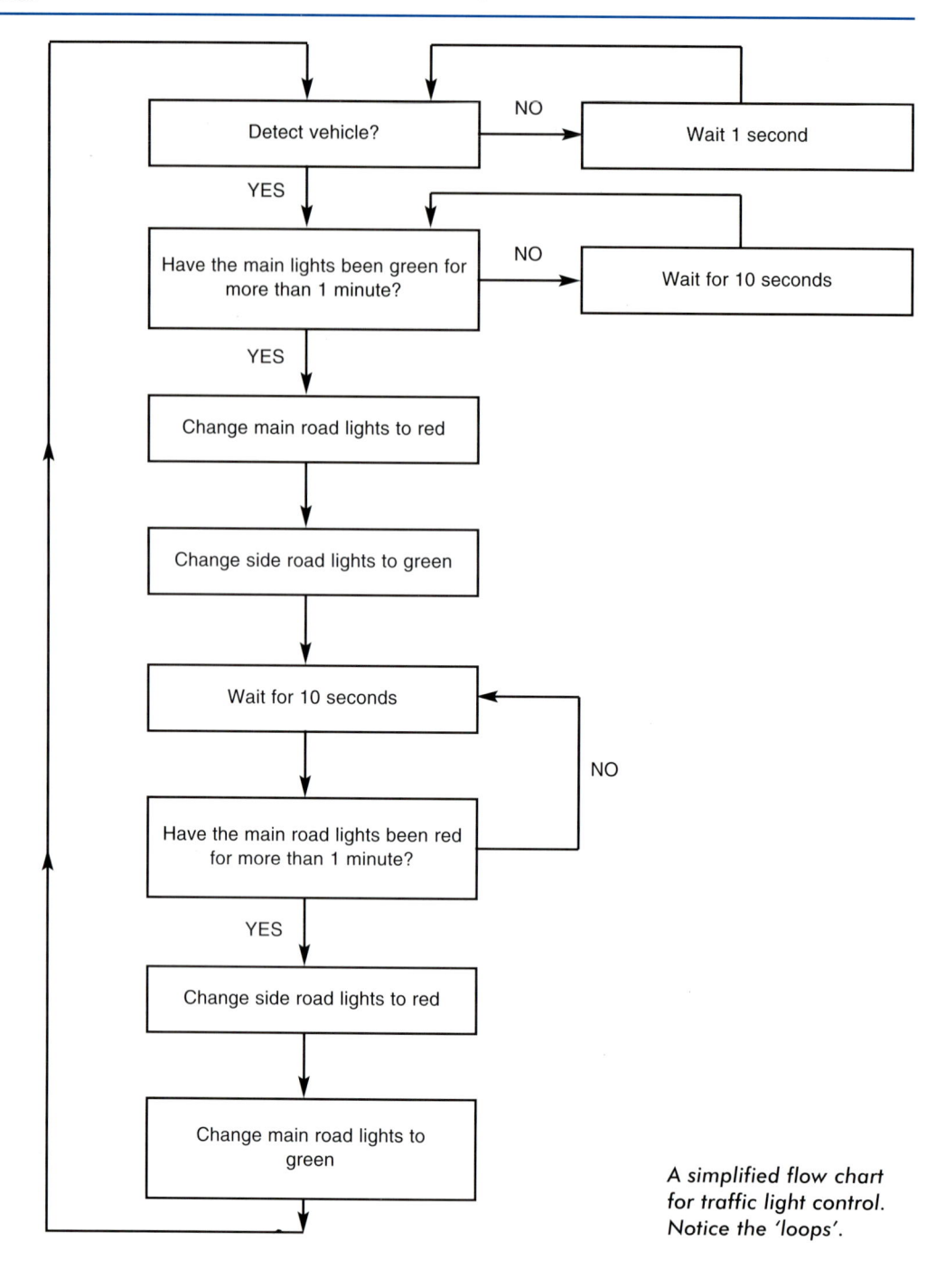

```
         ┌─────────────────────┐  NO   ┌─────────────────────┐
    ┌───▶│   Detect vehicle?   │──────▶│    Wait 1 second    │
    │    └─────────────────────┘       └─────────────────────┘
    │              │ YES                          │
    │              ▼                              │
    │    ┌─────────────────────┐  NO   ┌─────────────────────┐
    │    │ Have the main lights│──────▶│  Wait for 10 seconds│
    │    │ been green for more │       └─────────────────────┘
    │    │   than 1 minute?    │
    │    └─────────────────────┘
    │              │ YES
    │              ▼
    │    ┌─────────────────────┐
    │    │ Change main road    │
    │    │ lights to red       │
    │    └─────────────────────┘
    │              │
    │              ▼
    │    ┌─────────────────────┐
    │    │ Change side road    │
    │    │ lights to green     │
    │    └─────────────────────┘
    │              │
    │              ▼
    │    ┌─────────────────────┐
    │    │ Wait for 10 seconds │◀──┐
    │    └─────────────────────┘   │
    │              │               │
    │              ▼               │ NO
    │    ┌─────────────────────┐   │
    │    │ Have the main road  │───┘
    │    │ lights been red for │
    │    │  more than 1 minute?│
    │    └─────────────────────┘
    │              │ YES
    │              ▼
    │    ┌─────────────────────┐
    │    │ Change side road    │
    │    │ lights to red       │
    │    └─────────────────────┘
    │              │
    │              ▼
    │    ┌─────────────────────┐
    │    │ Change main road    │
    │    │ lights to green     │
    │    └─────────────────────┘
    │              │
    └──────────────┘
```

A simplified flow chart for traffic light control. Notice the 'loops'.

> Continue with the computer

Unit N: *Computers in Daily Life*

## USING CARDS TO GET CASH

Cash machines are used by bank customers to get money from the bank at any time. As long as the bank's computer is working, the cash machine will operate.

People who get money from a cash machine will have been given a *Personal Identification Number* – or PIN number. This is known only to the bank and their customer.

Each customer slides their *cash card* into the cash machine and then types in their PIN. The bank's computer does a *security check* to make sure the information on the card and the PIN match, then it provides cash or performs other functions such as providing a balance or ordering a new cheque book.

*Using a cash machine.*

### Using cards in shops

Bank cards are also used to pay for goods in shops. The shop takes the bank card and puts it through a small computerised machine connected to a telephone line. This sends information to the customer's bank. Cash is moved from the customer's bank account to the shop's bank account.

*A bank card being used in a shop.*

Unit N: *Computers in Daily Life*

## No cards *and* no cash!

Some banks enable their customers to operate their accounts from home. For example payments can be made without leaving home. Using your own computer you can call your bank's computer. It asks for your PIN and makes some other security checks. After this check you can send cash straight from your bank account to other people's bank accounts.

*Money can be sent straight from one person's bank account to another person's – without leaving home.*

## How many customers?

Shops may want to know how many customers visit the shop but don't buy anything. One way to do this is to use a simple *data logger* on the entry doors. As each person enters the shop they go through an infra-red beam of light. They 'break' the beam of light – and the data logger shows one more person has entered the shop.

At the end of the day the shop manager matches the number of customers who paid at the check-out tills, with the number counted by the data logger. The difference between the numbers shows how many people **didn't** buy anything.

## Barcodes

Goods on sale in most big shops and supermarkets have a *barcode* on them. When a customer takes goods to the check-out, the barcode on each is read by a beam of laser light. From this barcode data the computer in the check-out till knows the price and description of each item.

*The barcode gives information for the shop's computer.*

The item and its price is added to the total bill. Barcodes also enable shops to keep a check on their stocks of goods.

## The police and computers

The police use computers for a wide range of purposes.

Unit N: *Computers in Daily Life*

*The roadside camera's computer works out the speed of the passing vehicle. It just takes pictures of those vehicles going too fast.*

For example, computer-controlled cameras are used to catch speeding drivers. As a vehicle goes past the camera, the camera's computer works out the vehicle's speed. If the speed is faster than the speed limit, a photograph is taken.

Back at the police station another computer is used to find out who owns the vehicle. Then a 'speeding fine' is sent automatically to the owner's address.

If the car has been reported stolen or the owner is wanted by the police this information is shown on the screen.

```
Continue with the computer
```

## COMPUTERS IN SCHOOLS AND COLLEGES

Computers are also used for a wide range of purposes in schools and colleges.

For example they can be used to store student data, such as each student's address, class, progress in each subject, etc.

The same database can be used to keep a record of students who have been late or absent, what reason was given, what the total absences for the whole class have been, etc.

Some schools use databases to allow them to record student achievement and to monitor progress.

Creating good timetables for staff and students is a complicated procedure. Computer programs can help.

### Computers in the classroom

Computers are being integrated into lessons in a wide range of ways, across all subjects. Unit P provides examples of good practice in what is a huge area of opportunity. *Keybytes for Teachers* is concerned with developing the core ICT skills necessary to allow these opportunities to be embraced.

## Video conferencing

Video conferencing with students in other schools and colleges was mentioned in Unit E. Science experiments can be seen and talked about. Project ideas and information can be swapped. English students can practise their French, German, Spanish, etc with students from countries around the world. Those other students can practise their English.

*Video conferencing is being used more and more in business and education.*

## Interactive whiteboards

Interactive whiteboards were also mentioned in Unit E and can be used by the teacher in front of the whole class.

The whiteboard is linked to a computer and can show everything that can be shown on a computer screen. But, using an electronic pen, the board can be drawn on by the teacher. The finished work can be saved onto the computer's disk and printed if needed. These boards offer a wide range of facilities for specific subjects, e.g. the building of diagrams, step-by-step, in biology.

## Computers in the library

Computers are used in libraries to find books and to keep track of who has borrowed each book; and when! The details of all library members are stored in the computer.

When you borrow a book the librarian types in your name and scans the bar code on the book. The computer then works out which book you are borrowing and when it will be due back.

When you return the book the librarian scans the bar code again. The computer records are updated. If you return a book late the computer can automatically inform the librarian that a fine needs to be paid.

*A bar code on a book. The bars are read by a scanner and, from this, the book's author, title and subject are found by the library's computer.*

## Information – CD-ROM and the Internet

Books take time to prepare and to print, so information in books is soon out of date. Even if the book is re-published every year the information in it might still be two or more years old.

It is much quicker to prepare information and keep it up-to-date if it is published as a CD-ROM and information published on the Internet can be updated daily if necessary.

Libraries keep lots of CD-ROMs. Most of these come from publishers who have done proper research and have a good reputation. However some may be out of date.

The Internet can be used to find current information. ***But take care!*** There are hundreds of thousands of very good Internet addresses. On most of these the information is accurate and up to date. But some have been badly researched, and others are set up to ***deliberately mislead.***

It may be helpful to check all Internet or CD-ROM information against the following list:

- Is it from a Government department or from a well known publisher?

- Does the publisher's name or address give a clue to their interest? (For example the Health Education Department of the UK Government is much more likely to give good advice on smoking and health than information from unknown people called Tobacco Growers Marketing Inc.)

- What is the date of the book or CD-ROM or the 'last update' date on the Internet site?

Unit N: *Computers in Daily Life*

- Is the information complete? Many reports and directories will only include information from people who pay to be included.

- Does the book, CD-ROM, Internet site tell you how the information was collected? If it does you might be able to double-check some of the information against another book, CD-ROM, Internet site to make sure it is correct.

```
Continue with the computer
```

## COMPUTERS IN TOYS

Many toys use tiny computers. For example, a 'talking' spelling machine can be used by children to test their spelling of a range of words. The machine indicates if their spelling is right or wrong.

Other toys contain more powerful computers, e.g. games machines have very good graphics and are fast too!

```
Continue with the computer
```

## WELL – HANG ME!

The hangman game has been played with pencil and paper for years and years. We've played against the computer and looked at how the program works.

On the following page is a copy of the flow chart used to plan the game. The simple flow chart has four 'loops'. Each one tests for something. Then it 'loops' round and tests again, and again, and again …

Unit N: *Computers in Daily Life*

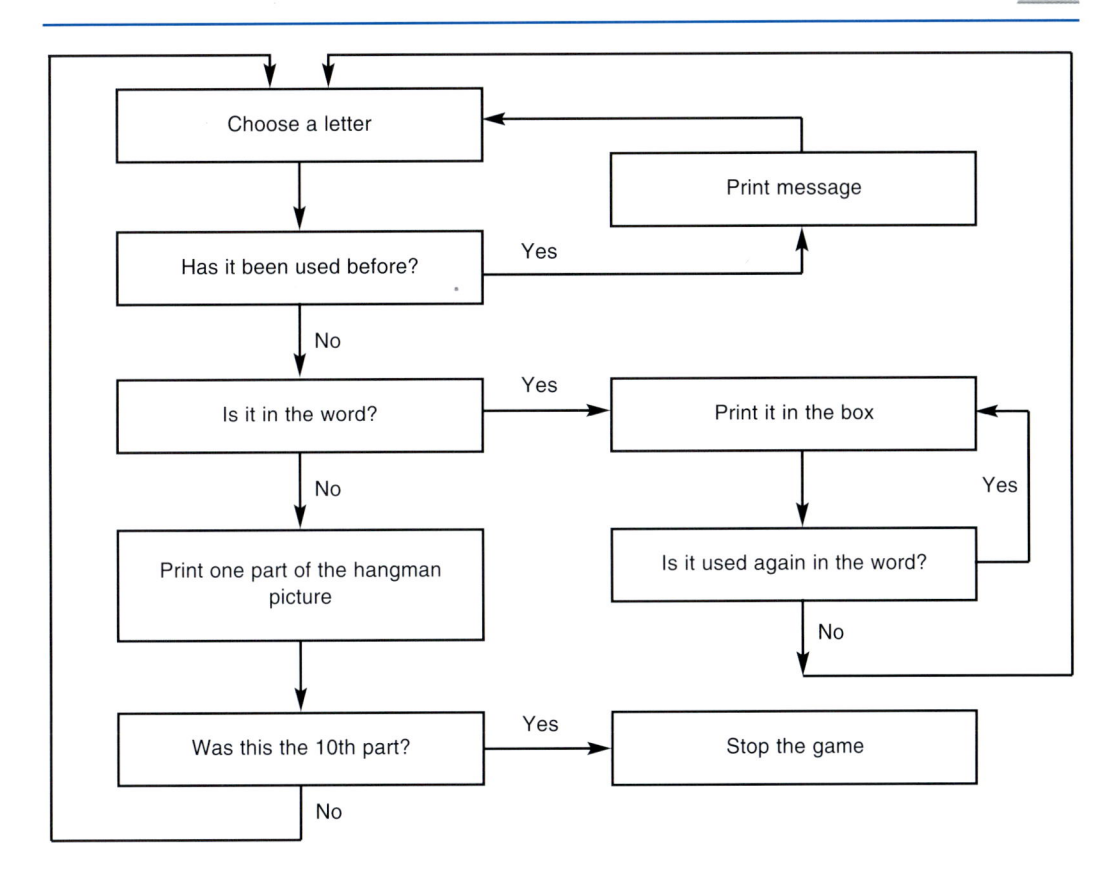

```
                    ┌──────────────────┐
                    │  Choose a letter │◄─────────────────┐
                    └────────┬─────────┘                  │
                             │        ┌───────────────┐   │
                             │        │ Print message │   │
                             ▼   Yes  └───────▲───────┘   │
                    ┌──────────────────┐      │           │
                    │ Has it been used │──────┘           │
                    │     before?      │                  │
                    └────────┬─────────┘                  │
                             │ No                         │
                             │        Yes ┌─────────────────────┐
                             ▼     ┌─────►│  Print it in the box │◄──┐
                    ┌──────────────────┐  └──────────┬──────────┘    │
                    │ Is it in the word?│─┘           │               │
                    └────────┬─────────┘              │          Yes  │
                             │ No                     ▼               │
                    ┌──────────────────┐   ┌─────────────────────┐    │
                    │ Print one part   │   │ Is it used again    │────┘
                    │ of the hangman   │   │    in the word?     │
                    │    picture       │   └──────────┬──────────┘
                    └────────┬─────────┘              │ No
                             │                        ▼
                             │     Yes    ┌─────────────────────┐
                             ▼    ┌──────►│    Stop the game    │
                    ┌──────────────────┐  └─────────────────────┘
                    │ Was this the     │─┘
                    │    10th part?    │
                    └────────┬─────────┘
                             │ No
```

*This simple flow chart shows how the hangman program can be made.*

┌─────────────────────────────────────────────┐
│         Continue with the computer          │
└─────────────────────────────────────────────┘

## SUMMARY SUMMARY SUMMARY SUMMARY SUMMARY

- Tiny computers are inside many types of equipment. The computer controls how the equipment works.

- Cars use a small computer to monitor and control the engine. Computers also give information to the driver.

- Traffic lights use sensors and are computer controlled to make sure the traffic keeps flowing smoothly.

141

Unit N: *Computers in Daily Life*

## SUMMARY SUMM

- The small computer in a fax machine turns the digital information from the telephone line into printed information.
- Some bank customers can move money by using their own computer to pay bills. First though a number of security checks will be made.
- A personal identification number (or PIN) is issued by the bank to each customer to be used as part of the security checking process.
- Computerised data logging helps shopkeepers know how many customers visit the shop and bar codes allow shops to keep accurate records of stock levels and sales.
- The police can detect speeding drivers using computer-controlled cameras and then automatically send the notice of the fine.
- Schools and colleges use computers for information about each student, their progress and their attendance records etc.
- Video conferencing and interactive whiteboards are useful teaching and learning tools.
- A good method of research is to use CD-ROM and the Internet. The information is more up to date than most books but careful checks should be made on how good the information is! Is it accurate, up to date, complete, true?
- The hangman flow chart shows how program 'loops' work to repeat an operation time after time.

**TASK** Consider how what you have learned in *KeyBytes* about word processing, databases, spreadsheets, graphics and desktop publishing can help you in your daily work as a teacher. Pages 161–171 and 173–181 suggest strategies for helping you integrate ICT into your classroom priorities.

# Unit 0

# Communications

## INTRODUCTION

Communication is about the 'exchange of information'.

The simplest way to communicate is to speak with someone face to face. Where this is not possible, because of distance, or for another reason, then the post, fax machines, phones, and computers can be used to overcome the difficulties.

Computers connect to phone lines through a modem allowing communication to take place. The modem makes it possible for the computer to send, or to get data from any other computer – anywhere in the world.

This unit explores computer communication in more detail: networks, intranets, e-mail, the Internet and the World Wide Web.

### Objectives

In this unit you will:

- learn why local area networks and wide area networks are now so prevalent and so useful in schools and colleges.
- consider the security requirements relating to networks.
- practise sending and receiving e-mail messages and understand the communication process relating to e-mails.
- learn how to search an intranet and the Internet and consider the role of each in your school or college.

Unit O: *Communications*

**Key words**

All subjects have their own specialised words which provide a shorthand means of communication. Lots of 'jargon' is used when people talk about networks and the Internet. This is just a small selection.

| | |
|---|---|
| **Access rights** | Networks are set up with security passwords so that each person can only use the files they have *access rights* to. |
| | Most people on a network only use some of the computer files. So users only need access rights to some of the files. |
| **Log on** | Means 'connect to', as in 'Log on to your Internet service provider' |
| **Attach** | To fix one thing to another. Any file can be attached to an e-mail. |
| **Remote access** | Means *log on* to the computer network by modem from a different place. |
| | For example, a sales representative may get information from his base office by *remote access* from his hotel each night. |
| **Fax** | A method of sending printed messages using the telephone lines. |
| **Voice messaging** | This works like an answerphone. Each person on a network can have *voice messages* left ready for them on their own computer. |
| **Hypertext** | Clicking on the hypertext word allows you to jump to the next part of the document. |
| | A hypertext word is linked to another part of the document by a *hyperlink*. |
| **Hotlinks** | Another word for hyperlinks. |
| **Download** | Copy a file from the Internet onto your own computer. |
| **Web site** | A collection of web pages – all linked by hyperlinks. |
| **Surf the net** | Search around the Internet by using hyperlinks, hotlinks, hypertext links to move around a whole lot of web sites. |
| **Hits** | Each time a web site is looked at it *scores a hit*! |

Unit O: *Communications*

> Continue with the computer

## NETWORKS

A network is a set of computers connected together.

### Local Area Networks

The smallest possible network is two computers linked by a network cable. Each computer connects to the network cable through a ***network card*** which is inside the base unit of each 'networked' computer.

This type of network is a ***local area network*** (LAN). LANs have been common in secondary schools for some years and are now becoming common in primary schools.

If more than five or six computers are in the local area network, an extra computer called ***the server*** is used to 'serve up' the files needed by all the other computers. The server also keeps all data free of error, and safely backed up.

Some systems have hundreds, even thousands, of networked computers on a single local area network. Schools or colleges may have a hundred or more.

*A network card. Each computer on a LAN is connected to the network cable through a card like this. The card fits into the base unit.*

### Wide Area Networks

A ***wide area network*** (WAN) will link computers in different parts of the country, or different parts of the world. Modems are used to connect the distant computers on the network. This connection can be through the telephone system or may use another high-speed link such as microwave or satellite.

Unit O: *Communications*

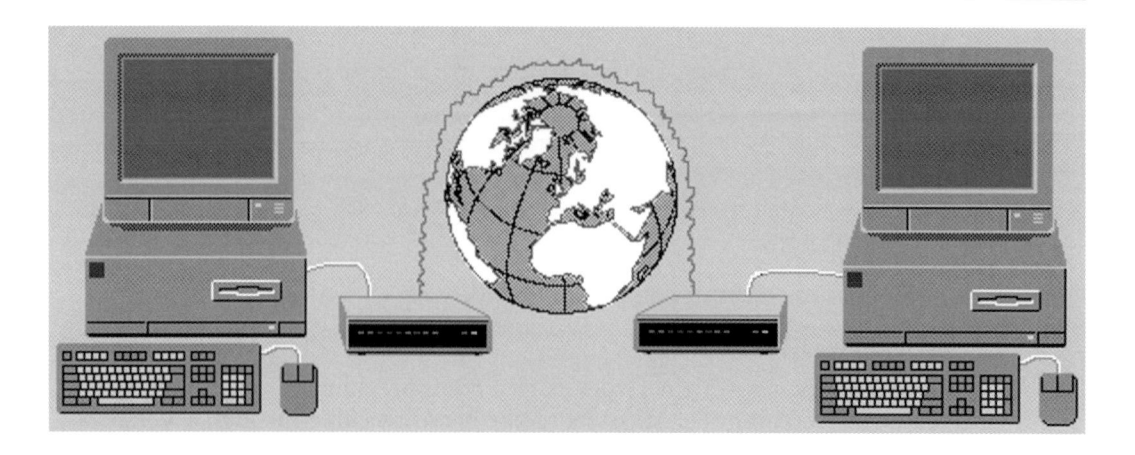

Banks use wide area networks. This allows someone from (say) Aberdeen in Scotland to withdraw money from a cash machine in Boston in the USA.

The Boston cash machine calls the bank's main computer (which may be in Edinburgh). The main computer has all the details of the person's account. The main computer then tells the cash machine in Boston whether to give money or to refuse.

This is an example of how computer communication can be done instantly via satellite and microwave links over a WAN.

*Satellites are used for worldwide computer communications.*

### Why are networks needed?

On a network, copying programs and data from one computer to another is quick and easy. There's no need to use floppy disks.

All data stored on any computer on a network can be *shared*. So all the files on the server or any of the other connected computers can be used by everyone else on the network. This is useful in schools and colleges as documents which a number of teachers need, e.g. schemes of work, standard letters, policies, can be placed on the network and are then always available.

Hardware such as printers, scanners, modems and even hard disks can also be shared by everyone on the network.

## Why share data?

If all the people who need information use the same database then lots of work and errors can be avoided.

Imagine the confusion if all the travel agents around the country used their own holiday-booking databases. They would never be quite sure whether their data was up to date. So they wouldn't know if the holiday you wanted to book was still actually available.

To stop this happening they use a single database and are all linked to it on a WAN.

## Who has access?

Some data on most networks is private. Before any of the data is shared with other computers, the files must be set up to allow the computers of other 'authorised' people to connect up and to be able to use the files. This is called setting up *access rights* to the files on the network.

The server can also be set up to allow different people different access rights. For example the Head of ICT will generally have full 'Administrator' rights; but a student will only have 'User' rights.

Each person who uses the network has their own security password. For example: the student version of *KeyBytes* is usually run on a school or college network. The *teachers'* network password will give them access rights to look at student end-of-unit test scores. But student access rights won't allow students to look at scores; so that the security of that information is protected.

---

**Continue with the computer**

---

## E-MAIL

E-mail stands for *electronic mail.* It's super fast, super cheap and often much more useful than post or fax.

Anyone on a LAN or WAN network can **send** and **receive** e-mails to everyone else on the same network.

Also, because the Internet links a huge number of computer networks together, you can e-mail anyone, wherever they are in the world, providing they are on the Internet.

E-mail is very popular, and there are good reasons for this.

- It's very quick. You don't have to write envelopes or wait for the post collection and delivery.

- Data such as word processor files and drawings can be 'attached' to the e-mail. This data comes straight from your computer – so you don't even need to print it before sending it.

- You don't have to be at your computer to receive an e-mail. New messages that arrive while you are away can be read as soon as you 'collect your mail' on the computer.

- E-mails are written less formally than conventional mail, which allows messages to be created and sent very rapidly.

### Dangers!

**E-mailing friends:** Work places often have policies about the e-mailing of friends in work time. E-mails are very often sent by friends who use their computer keyboards to 'chat'. They forget that e-mail communication *isn't always private*! E-mails can be printed – by your boss and anyone else with approved access. So don't chat about things which you do not want made public.

It is also wise not to respond too quickly to e-mails which upset or annoy you.

**E-mailing other people:** Write an e-mail in the same style you would a letter to the person. Teachers should be just as careful e-mailing parents and students as they would be if they were writing a letter. School policy should spell out procedures and the acceptability of teacher/parent e-mails.

A teacher of several hundred students in a secondary school will not have the time to keep in e-mail contact with many parents.

### E-mail across the Internet

You can keep in touch with friends and colleagues all around the world by e-mail. Teachers and students in different countries now undertake joint projects using e-mail to exchange photos and documents and to ask questions.

In order for you to send and receive e-mail, your computer must be connected to the Internet, e.g. through a telephone system via a modem. Then you need to choose an Internet 'service provider'. There are hundreds of these; some make you pay for the service, others may give the service free. You may find your school gets a special deal through a government approved provider.

Once you have loaded the service provider's program and are connected to them you will be given an 'e-mail address'. This address is in three parts:

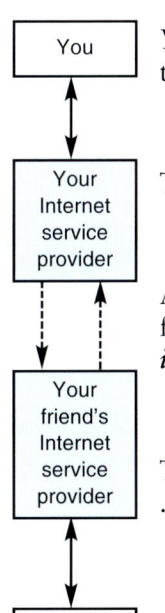

*Your name* – in the way you want it (unless someone is already using that).

Debbs

The symbol for '*at*' followed by the name of the **service provider.**

Debbs@freeserve

A full stop then the '*type*' of service, e.g. 'co' or 'com' for company, 'gov' for government, 'sch' for school – another full stop and the *country initials.*

Debbs@freeserve.co.uk

The last part isn't always exactly like this; some service providers just use .com others .net etc. For example:

Debbs@aol.com

Debbs@kuwait.net

You → Your Internet service provider → Your friend's Internet service provider → Your friend

Unit O: Communications

Once you and your friends or colleagues in other schools have their own addresses you can e-mail each other. Your e-mails go from your computer to your service provider. Your service provider sends it on to your friend's (or colleague's) service provider. When they next log on to the Internet they can collect your e-mail.

Their reply will be sent back to your service supplier (through your contact's service provider). So, when you log on later the same day you might have an answer! There are ways of working offline to avoid expensive phone calls. Ask your service provider for details.

### Attaching files to an e-mail

Data files can be sent with an e-mail. Pictures, sound, programs, documents – they can all be 'attached' to the message.

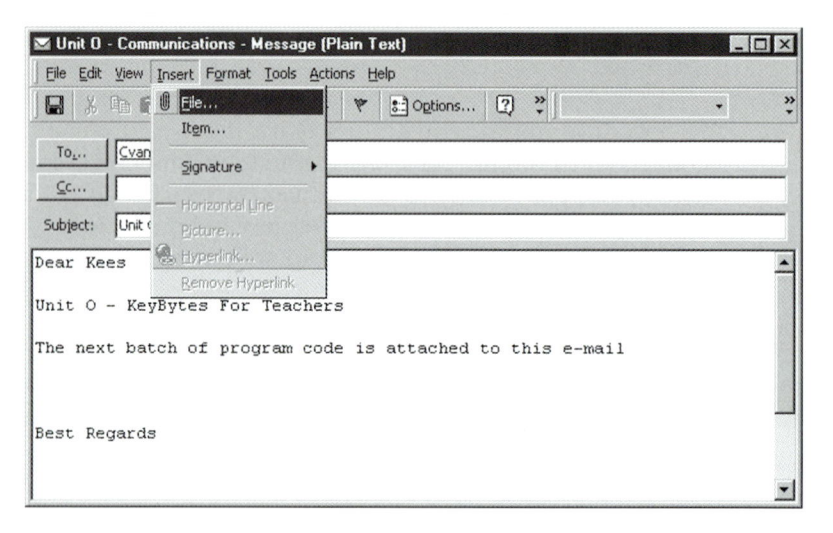

*The KeyBytes programming was done partly in England and partly in Holland. Data files were attached to e-mails almost every day.*

It's a very simple job to attach a file. It is because of this facility that e-mail use has so quickly overtaken fax use. Datafiles can't be attached to faxes that are sent by, or received by, an ordinary fax machine.

```
Continue with the computer
```

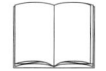

## WIDE AREA NETWORKS. FAX AND VOICE MESSAGES

### Modems

Everyone using a wide area network (WAN) or the Internet needs some type of modem. The word 'modem' is a contraction of the description of the device – 'modulator-demodulator'.

Modems change the binary code used by computers (the code of zeros and ones) into a code used by telephone systems. They also do the opposite. When a modem receives information through a telephone system it turns it back into binary code so it can be understood by the receiving computer.

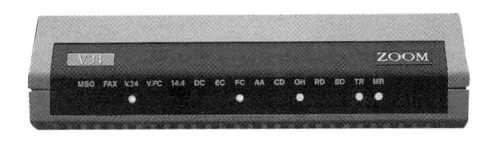

High-speed modems can send and receive data very quickly. If you have a high-speed modem or a high speed ISDN telephone line your WAN will work much faster and the telephone charges will be lower.

Some modems are very small and fit inside a desktop, laptop and even palmtop computers. Others are larger and sit alongside the computer. The important characteristic of a modem is its speed.

Modems are useful in many different ways. Let's explore a few of these.

### Working on a wide area network

People like designers and software developers often work mainly from home. They find they can work more quickly than in an office and save travel time. Teachers also find that certain sorts of work can be completed more efficiently at home.

Home working can be particularly effective when your computer is linked to others on the school's wide area network. You can then use all the programs and files on the WAN and your work is saved on the server, just as though you were using a computer in the school building. The modem might be continually busy – or just when a new file is wanted or a file needs to be saved.

When people work at home with a computer and modem it is called *teleworking*.

Teachers use home computers for many professional purposes. When using electronic documents, the teacher can connect their laptop or home computer to the network to send or receive files and messages from colleagues and students.

The use of a school or college network in this way is called ***remote access***.

## Unit O: Communications

*Teleworking: working at home using the company's wide area network.*

### Telelearning

Computers and modems can enable remote learning. With remote learning students can be tutored by specialist teachers many miles away.

Each student has a computer and modem. The teacher sends the student each day's work. When the work is done the student sends it back to the teacher. Exams can even be taken via the computer. Where groups of students in remote areas cannot all meet in one place, video conferencing plus e-mail is used for tuition.

*Telelearning* is useful in countries where it may be hundreds of kilometres to the nearest teacher, such as in Australia, Norway or Sweden. Also it's useful where a student wants to learn a subject which has very few teachers.

### Fax and voice messages

*Fax announcement*

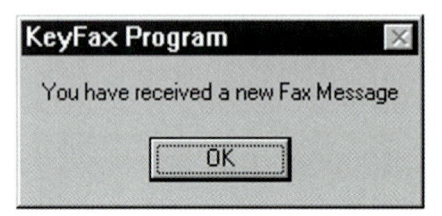

Strange as it may seem, you don't need a fax machine to send and receive faxes. You can do this with a computer, modem and a fax program. When you receive a fax through a modem it appears on the screen, not on paper. You can print it later, if you want to.

Sending a fax with a computer and modem is easy. You prepare the message on the screen, then send it. There's no need to print it out first and feed it into the fax machine.

A computer and modem can also be used to record voice messages.

```
Continue with the computer
```

Unit O: Communications

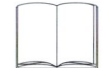

# INTRANETS

## What's an intranet?

We've already seen some of the things that can be done on the *Internet*. But this section is about *intranets*. Intranets are different – but similar!

We will use the example of a company intranet to describe how the intranet works and what it can help people to do.

Imagine you're the sales manager for a big builder's merchants. Your company sells thousands and thousands of different sorts of building, plumbing, and decorating supplies to builders, plumbers, decorators, etc.

Each month you are visited by representatives of all your suppliers – they have leaflets about their new products, and changes to others. How can you and your staff keep track with what you can buy, what you can sell and what you have in stock?

Well, you have an intranet. With this you can all keep up to date at all times.

Each new leaflet left by a supplier is scanned into a DTP program. A *hypertext* heading is put on the page and hyperlinks are made to other related pages and to a database which holds the price and stock information on all the products the company sells.

The whole document – which is thousands of pages long – is on the company's network server. ***This huge document is the company's intranet.***

Any person who works for the company can quickly find information about every product. They carry out a search on the company's intranet.

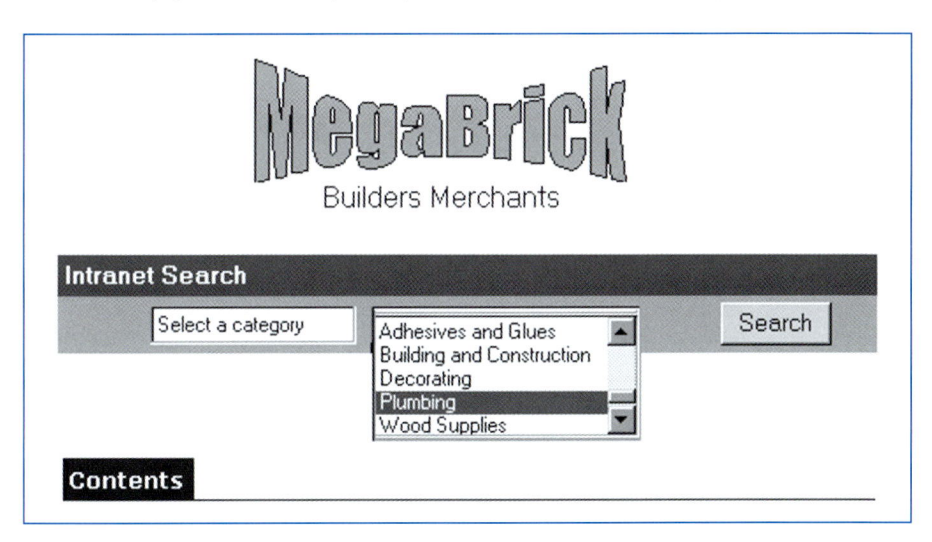

**MegaBrick**
Builders Merchants

**Intranet Search**

| Select a category | Adhesives and Glues
Building and Construction
Decorating
Plumbing
Wood Supplies | Search |

**Contents**

153

# Unit O: Communications

## Searching an intranet

A customer wants a special sort of tap for a bathroom hand-basin. The search might be:

First part of the search ⟶ Plumbing

Next part of the search ⟶ Central Heating
Bathrooms
Kitchens

Last part of the search ⟶ Taps – Brass
Taps – Chrome
Taps – Stainless Steel

So the search has very rapidly narrowed down to just the few pages of bathroom chrome taps.

The customer looks at the DTP page with its picture of the product and decides he wants two 'Superflash' taps.

A single click on another hyperlink and the 'stock record' for Superflash taps appears on the screen. This shows there are three in stock – and they are in the warehouse stock location number H54.

**Stock Record**

Superflash taps

| 3 | H54 |
|---|---|
| Number | Location |

So intranets are like huge catalogues or directories – with links to any number of files. The reason to have an intranet is to be sure that *everyone* on the network can get accurate information *all the time*.

## How to search

Start by trying one or two words that describe what you want. For example 'taps' or 'bath taps'. If this takes you in the right direction – then usually you get a choice which 'narrows down' the search.

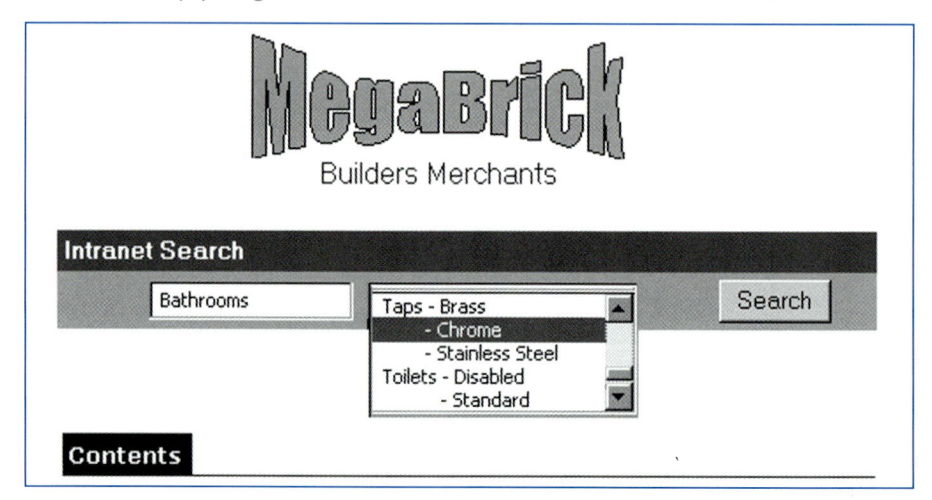

**MegaBrick**
Builders Merchants

**Intranet Search**

Bathrooms | Taps - Brass / - Chrome / - Stainless Steel / Toilets - Disabled / - Standard | Search

Contents

Unit O: *Communications*

Many schools and colleges are now developing intranets which are used to store resources for lessons in every subject area, as well as to make records of field trips and social events available to the whole school.

### Searching CD-ROMs

Multimedia encyclopedias on CD-ROMs use the same type of search process. In many ways they are like a mini-intranet!

```
Continue with the computer
```

## THE WORLD WIDE WEB – 'the Web'

The World Wide Web is a vast multimedia information store. It's like a gigantic Intranet – but instead of data being stored on just one network it's *hundreds of thousands of networks all joined together.* The information is described as 'multimedia' because it combines different media, ie text, graphics, sound and perhaps video clips.

Hundreds of thousands of different companies, individuals and organisations put information onto web pages.

Anyone who has an Internet service provider connection can use almost all of the web pages. Lots of them are about educational resources, or companies' products, or places to visit, or famous people, or world affairs, or travel information, or sport and hobbies, or music, or films, or ... almost any topic you can imagine.

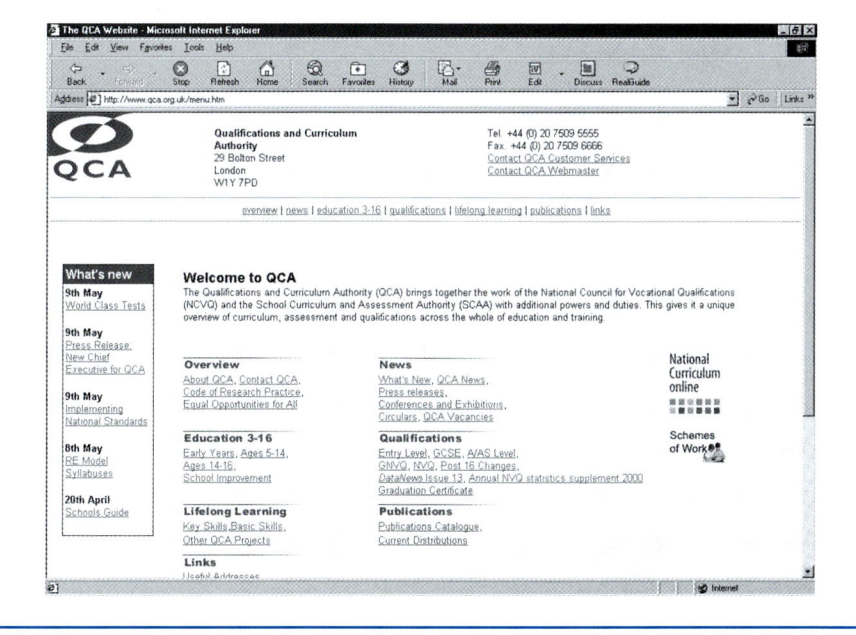

*Some World Wide Web pages are just text – but many have lots of pictures and some have video and sound.*

You can find out about anything you choose on the Web. Day or night, wherever you are the Web provides access to a huge store of information.

On most web pages the information is free. Usually you have to pay the telephone connection charge at a 'local rate' for the time you are connected. There is a charge on some web sites. Also make sure you disconnect your modem when you have finished.

### Downloading

Some web pages let you *download* programs, such as government documents, educational resources, games or trial software (software that has a life of, say, four weeks).

Downloading is the process of copying programs or data onto your own computer. In some cases you also need to pay for the program before downloading it. You can do this by supplying a bank card number.

Again – more warnings! Download programs may contain *viruses* – so always virus scan them before using them. Also bank card numbers given on the Internet can possibly be 'stolen' by computer experts – so be warned. Use reputable sites only. These will make it clear who is providing the information.

### Quality of Web information

Many web pages are very valuable. They give accurate, well researched, up-to-date information free to anyone who 'visits' the web site.

Some web pages are misleading. They give *out-of-date* information, or information that is simply *wrong*. Sometimes this is deliberate. Students need to be taught how to evaluate the quality and provenance of web sites.

### Web Addresses

Every web page has its own address. Usually though, all we need is the *home page* address. This is like the title page in a book. Hyperlinks lead from the home page into all other pages on that web site.

If you know the home page address – then click on File, then Open, then just type in the address and press the *Search* button.

All World Wide Web addresses look something like this:

> http://www.sitename.com

You don't need to type the 'http://' bit in – but the rest must be completely accurate.

Unit O: *Communications*

---

> Continue with the computer

## SURFING AND SHOPPING

It's quite fun to 'surf the net'. Often you start out looking for one web site and end up looking at many others because there are so many interesting hotlinks. However, it is also all too easy to surf without finding much of value. Teacher associations will often recommend sites and pages 161–171 explore this topic more fully.

There are however lots of web sites where you can download files or programs.

*Music files* (called MP3 files) can be downloaded and played. Always read the copyright notices on these and obey the rules.

Government and other organisations have lots of large reports that can be downloaded as document files.

Downloadable programs are usually trial-software and small updates to existing programs which you can get for free.

### Searching on the Web

Often you don't know a web site address that will have what you need. So you need to find all the sites that might be about the topic you are interested in. You must do a *search*.

Try typing in http://www.yahoo.com. This is the address of one search engine which will look for sites on a given topic.

Once you type in the word, or words you want to search for, the Web Search program goes to work. When it has looked through all its data it gives a list of web sites that match your search words. There might be only a few sites, or there might be thousands.

If there are more than about 20 sites try a new search – use a different word that more exactly fits what you want.

For example: if you search on: 'Museums and art galleries' you'll get thousands of hits. Too many to research.

Change the search to: 'the Louvre' and you only get a manageable number of hits. Then you can begin to look at these web sites one-by-one.

Just click on the hyperlink to each site, one at a time. You may soon find useful information. If you want to print it, go to File on the Menu bar; then Print.

## Offensive material on the Web

Students will very quickly learn to search for subjects you and their parents would prefer them not to research! Occasionally it is possible they will innocently chance across a site that is at least modestly pornographic – but this will be an exception. Mainly, sites which most people will find offensive must be specifically searched for; so don't be too easily convinced of the 'innocent' explanation.

There are a growing number of 'family friendly' filters offered by the Internet service providers and Search Sites. These will exclude sites which contain keywords suggestive of pornography, racism, violence, etc. Also there is other third party software that can be used and which is purpose-designed for school or college use across the network such as: www.netnanny.co.uk

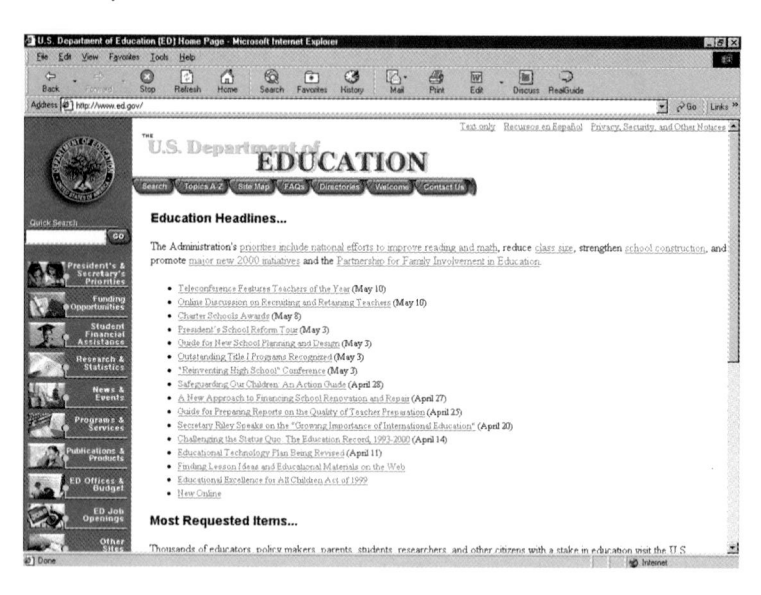

*US Dept. of Education web site*

Many governments provide educational sites. Although not all of these are in English free translation software is regularly advertised as a service by some of the Internet service providers.

## E-Commerce

If you don't live near a big town, or hate tramping around the shops, then the Internet can bring the shops to you.

Companies have set up web sites to sell all types of goods. Books, educational resources, music CDs, computer hardware, computer software and insurance are the most popular choices. But 'everything and anything' can be found for sale somewhere on the Internet.

Payment is made by typing in your bank card details. Then, *if all goes well*, the goods are delivered a few days later.

Unit O: Communications

There are some dangers with buying goods over the Internet. Here are two:

- Your bank card details might be stolen by someone else on the Internet.
- The goods might not arrive.

Remember that anyone can set up a web site and offer goods for sale. Be sure you trust the company you think you are dealing with. Are they well known? Do they give an address that you can check? Do you know anyone who has dealt with them already?

If the company is reliable they will have protected their web site so that it is very difficult for your bank card details to be stolen.

Companies who sell things over the Internet don't need High Street shops. They have millions and millions of people who can become customers; not just those who live in a single town. So their prices can be expected to be lower than High Street prices.

> Continue with the computer

## SUMMARY SUMMARY SUMMARY SUMMARY SUMMARY

- A network is a set of connected computers.
- Some networks use an extra computer called a server to manage the files.
- There are two main kinds of network: local area networks (LANs) and wide area networks (WANs).
- LANs use cable to link the computers; WANs need modems.
- Networks allow data to be copied and shared quickly and easily.
- Data, programs and expensive hardware can be shared on a network.
- On a network different people are given different access rights. This allows some files to be kept private.
- E-mails are fast and quick. Anyone on the same network can be e-mailed.
- Take care to be polite when you e-mail – other people may read them!
- E-mailing can be done on the Internet if you have an Internet service provider and an e-mail address.
- Every sort of computer file can be sent attached to an e-mail. The receiver can read the message and download the files.

## Unit O: Communications

## SUMMARY

- Computers on a WAN communicate over satellite, microwave or telephone systems.
- Modems make teleworking, telelearning and remote access possible.
- Intranets are like huge catalogues of all types of data used by everyone on a company or institution's network. Each piece of data is linked to others with hyperlinks.
- Searching on intranets and the Internet is a useful skill.
- The World Wide Web is a huge collection of multimedia information pages that can be found on the Internet.
- Programs and files can be downloaded from the Internet. But some may contain viruses!
- Some information on the World Wide Web is very good. Some information is likely to be out of date or wrong.
- Web page addresses are usually for each site's home page. Hyperlinks then take you to all the other pages on the web site.
- Most files that can be downloaded are copyright. Read and obey the copyright notices.
- E-commerce lets you buy almost anything using the Internet. Take care that the company with whom you are dealing is honest.
- Often goods bought from companies selling on the Internet are cheaper than from a High Street shop.

## TASKS

1. Check that you can send e-mail and that you can attach documents to it. Colleagues or your service provider should be able to help. A point to note is that if your students are to learn to use ICT it is very important that in your school teachers feel able to ask each other for help. The nature of the technology means that we can all go on learning more and more about the software we use, and sharing knowledge with colleagues is one of the quickest ways to learn.

2. Explore the educational sites provided by your government – telephone the relevant organisation if you cannot find their site. Consider how the materials provided help you in your work. Explore the European Schoolnet site (http://www.eun.org). Much of this site is published in several languages.

3. Find out if teachers' professional organisations in your country have web sites of value to you.

# Using e-mail and the Internet in Your Teaching

*KeyBytes* has, among other things, introduced you to spreadsheets, databases, desktop publishing and, in the previous unit, the use of networks, e-mail and Internet. In this unit we focus on the educational applications of e-mail and Internet technology, giving examples of the application of the knowledge you have gained to your classroom practice and to your ongoing professional development.

## Objectives

In this unit you are introduced to:

- e-mail and Internet resources and projects.
- classroom management and lesson planning.
- use of Internet and e-mail for your own professional development.

```
This unit is a 'Coursebook-only' unit - so you
don't need to be at the computer to study it.
```

### E-MAIL AND INTERNET RESOURCES AND PROJECTS

The Internet provides *resources* – many of which are free – which teachers of a wide variety of subject areas find useful in lessons. The variable quality of web sites has been discussed in Unit O but there are many high quality educational sites produced by reputable organisations.

Many of the resources now available on the Internet would simply have been unobtainable or would not have become available for months or years if they had to be printed and distributed in book form. Examples of Internet resources that are available include:

- for *art*: web sites giving details of modern painters, art galleries showing aspects of their collections;

- for *history*: museum collections, collections of material relating to particular periods of development in different areas of the country – often collected by local universities and schools;

- for *geography*: materials about different regions, current weather charts, details about natural events such as earthquakes within hours of their occurrence;

- for *science*: links with laboratories and national organisations such as NASA and the professional association web site for the Association for Science Education (**http://www.ase.org.uk/**).

Reputable providers of such educational sites include governments, museums, art galleries, educational institutions, national broadcasting companies e.g. the BBC in the UK (**http://www.bbc.co.uk/**), the Australian Broadcasting Corporation in Australia (**http://www.abc.net.au/btn/**).

The worldwide availability of local and national newspapers and radio on the Web provides another resource for, for example, *English*, *economics*, *business studies*, or when viewed or listened to in the target languages pupils are studying, *modern foreign languages*. Search engines (such as **http://www.yahoo.com** or **http://www.altavista.com**) can be helpful to you in finding such sites. Media publications such as the *Times Educational Supplement Online, Education Guardian, Junior Education* are a good source of educational web site addresses. We also suggest you ask colleagues or professional associations for examples of sites they have found useful.

But the Internet also provides the opportunity to *communicate* – cheaply for many schools (this depends on the policies of telecommunications providers and national governments), synchronously and asynchronously. This means students doing project work or investigative work, which requires responses from students in other countries, can e-mail questions one day and expect replies within the next day or so. Communication projects, using the Internet and e-mail, provide one of the major new developments for schools which can be applied across subjects to curriculum work in both secondary and primary students.

### Projects using communication through the Internet

Video conferencing has been mentioned in a previous unit. Cheap video conferencing sets for use with PCs are within the budget of many schools (and indeed families). These can be successfully used to:

- prepare students for a school exchange;

- communicate with children in other cultures as part of a programme of study and research;

- link with museums such as the Science Museum in London where video-conferences are arranged for schools around the world so that students can see artefacts held in the museum, can talk to experts at the museum, can see demonstrations of experiments and equipment that are not available in their own school.

### The 'virtual' expert

There is considerable scope for building on this notion of 'the expert in the classroom': that is, bringing experts from industry and other backgrounds into the classroom through their on-screen presence. The idea can also be applied to e-mail exchanges. It may be that an expert in an area of the curriculum which you are teaching who is working in industry may agree to answer your students' e-mails about the topic being studied.

### Planning and managing a project and finding partners for projects

If you wish to undertake projects with other schools then there are a number of ways of finding partners. Some established educational sites offer this facility e.g. the European School Net site (**http://www.eun.org**) and the British Council Montage site (**http://www.bc.org.au/montage**) but there are many more. Ask colleagues if they know of other sites.

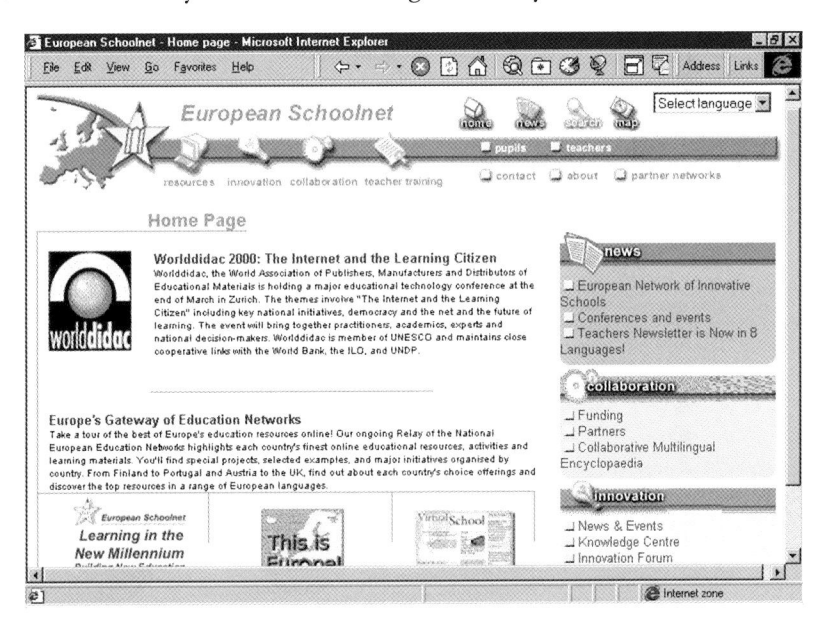

*Partner finding from the EUN site*

Unless you are joining a project advertised by another teacher, you need to plan your online project before you advertise for partners. A typical plan might include the headings below:

- Project title:
- Date: from — to —
- Educational objectives/Purpose:
- Subjects covered:
- Age range:

- Summary of project:
- Participants sought:
- Activities:
- Your contact details:

*Using e-mail and the Internet in Your Teaching*

The pictures which follow show examples of how partners and projects are advertised on both the European School Net and British Council Montage sites.

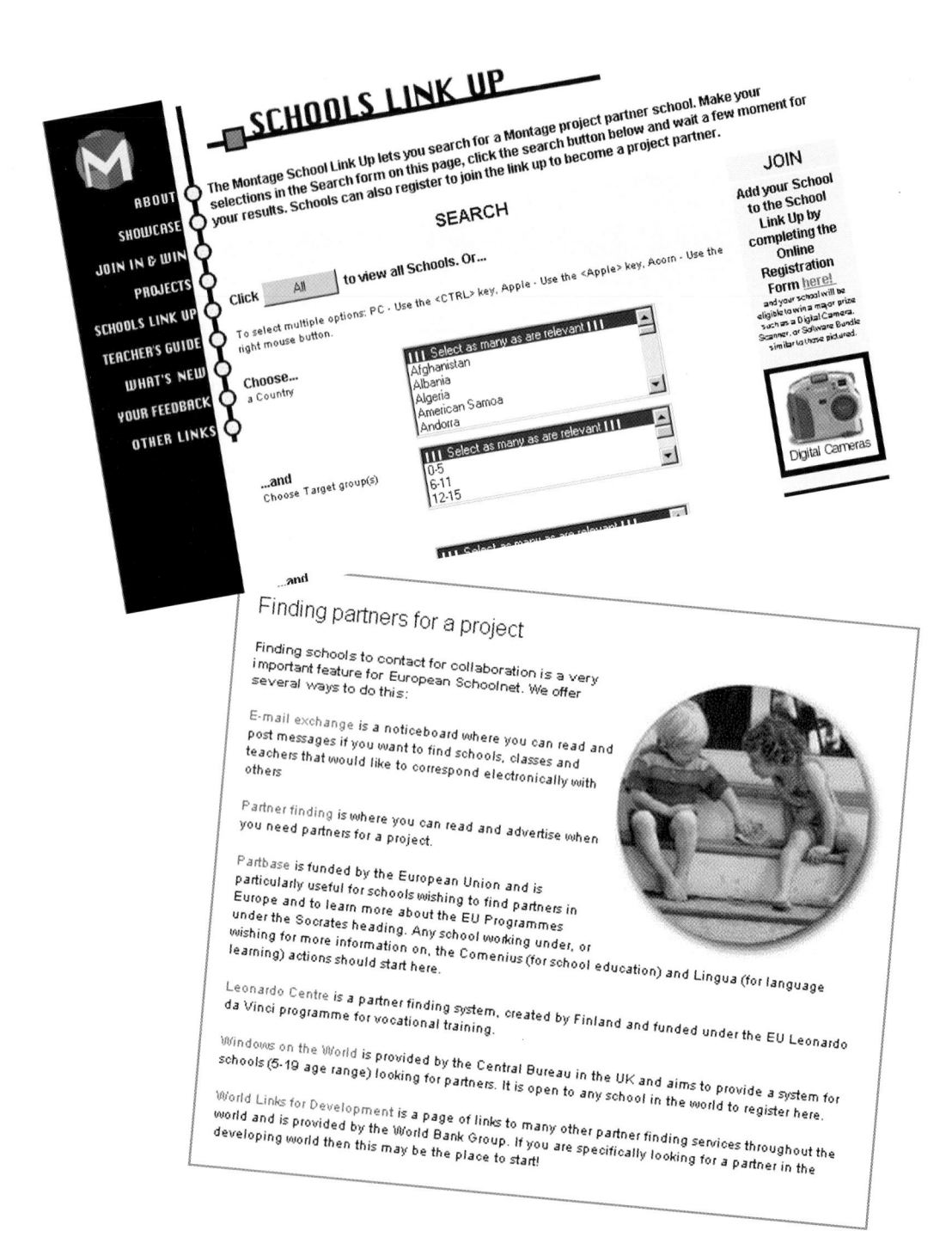

## SCHOOLS LINK UP

The Montage School Link Up lets you search for a Montage project partner school. Make your selections in the Search form on this page, click the search button below and wait a few moment for your results. Schools can also register to join the link up to become a project partner.

SEARCH

Click [ All ] to view all Schools. Or...

To select multiple options: PC - Use the <CTRL> key, Apple - Use the <Apple> key, Acorn - Use the right mouse button.

Choose...
a Country

!!! Select as many as are relevant !!!
Afghanistan
Albania
Algeria
American Samoa
Andorra

...and
Choose Target group(s)

!!! Select as many as are relevant !!!
0-5
6-11
12-15

ABOUT
SHOWCASE
JOIN IN & WIN
PROJECTS
SCHOOLS LINK UP
TEACHER'S GUIDE
WHAT'S NEW
YOUR FEEDBACK
OTHER LINKS

JOIN
Add your School to the School Link Up by completing the Online Registration Form here! and your school will be eligible to win a major prize such as a Digital Camera, Scanner, or Software Bundle similar to those pictured.

Digital Cameras

### Finding partners for a project

Finding schools to contact for collaboration is a very important feature for European Schoolnet. We offer several ways to do this:

E-mail exchange is a noticeboard where you can read and post messages if you want to find schools, classes and teachers that would like to correspond electronically with others

Partner finding is where you can read and advertise when you need partners for a project.

Partbase is funded by the European Union and is particularly useful for schools wishing to find partners in Europe and to learn more about the EU Programmes under the Socrates heading. Any school working under, or wishing for more information on, the Comenius (for school education) and Lingua (for language learning) actions should start here.

Leonardo Centre is a partner finding system, created by Finland and funded under the EU Leonardo da Vinci programme for vocational training.

Windows on the World is provided by the Central Bureau in the UK and aims to provide a system for schools (5-19 age range) looking for partners. It is open to any school in the world to register here.

World Links for Development is a page of links to many other partner finding services throughout the world and is provided by the World Bank Group. If you are specifically looking for a partner in the developing world then this may be the place to start!

Darren Leafe[1], a teacher of the upper primary age group describes the **'Where in Oz/UK'** project which his students in the UK undertook with students in Australia:

> "The **Where in Oz/UK** project was designed to reinforce a range of skills, to encourage and provide a meaningful purpose for research and to extend the students' knowledge of another country.
>
> ... It was proposed that an activity which involved the students examining the geography of their own country would achieve the objectives, develop a high level of motivation and provide opportunities for additional learning outcomes to be supported and encouraged. Most importantly, the use of communications technology was seen to be able to improve the quality and standard of the students' education by providing a context within which the objectives could be met.
>
> The project, therefore, had focused objectives which were directly related to the teachers' (curriculum) planning, allowed for a certain degree of flexibility as regards learning outcomes and used ICT as tool through which learning would take place.
>
> Working arrangements were established (with the Australian partner) and the following issues were addressed:
>
> - What were the students going to learn?
> - What were the students going to do?
> - What were the staff going to do?
> - How was the project going to be assessed?
>
> The students were to be taught the necessary geographical and ICT related skills which they would need before communications between the schools began. The project provided the context through which the objective was to be met, however, it was crucial that the skills that the students would need were identified and taught. The students' participation in the link provided opportunities for these skills to be reinforced and developed.
>
> The students at each school were expected to use their geographical skills to produce a number of clues which related to a major town in their country. This would then be e-mailed to the partner school where the students would use the appropriate skills to find the location. They were then expected to e-mail their answer back and wait for the reply.
>
> To begin the task, explicit teaching, modelling and discussion occurred. Destinations were selected by the students; groupings of students were negotiated; critical discussion and decision-making occurred in regard to the categories for the clues e.g. a natural

> feature, a tourist attraction, an historical event, a geographical feature such as a mountain, river, etc. Explicit teaching and modelling of appropriate language was necessary. Then the groups of students worked together to write their e-mails where the final and deciding clue was to be the latitude and longitude of the destination."

The **Travel Buddy** is another popular project for primary schools which teachers have successfully used to provide motivation for writing. This type of project is described fully on the British Council Montage site. A class chooses a stuffed toy (Travel Buddy) to represent their country and they send the Travel Buddy complete with materials about the school and country to another class in another country. Pupils in that country take it in turn to take the Travel Buddy home, e-mailing back to the home school about the activities the Travel Buddy 'experienced' the day before. Where possible, the classes exchange Travel Buddies so that both classes experience the writing and questioning activities.

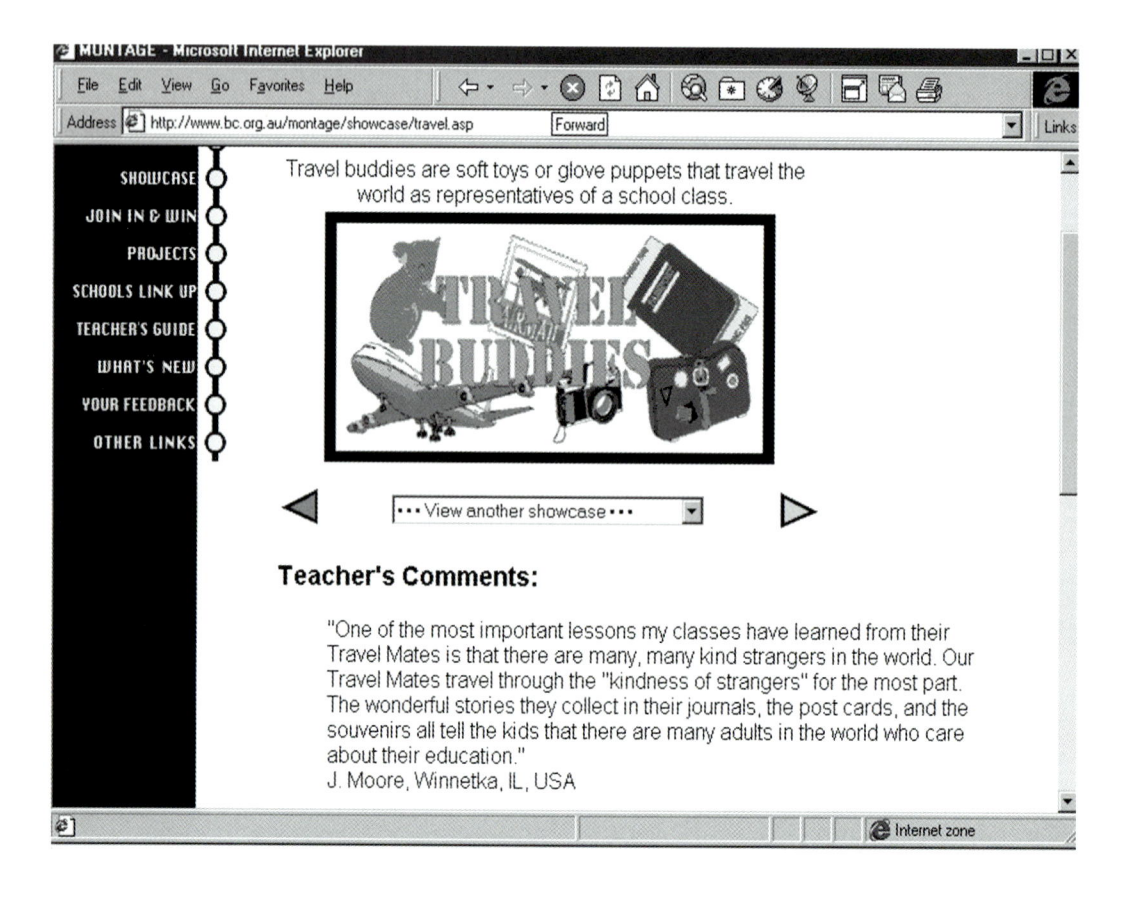

---

MONTAGE - Microsoft Internet Explorer

Address: http://www.bc.org.au/montage/showcase/travel.asp

- SHOWCASE
- JOIN IN & WIN
- PROJECTS
- SCHOOLS LINK UP
- TEACHER'S GUIDE
- WHAT'S NEW
- YOUR FEEDBACK
- OTHER LINKS

Travel buddies are soft toys or glove puppets that travel the world as representatives of a school class.

*** View another showcase ***

**Teacher's Comments:**

"One of the most important lessons my classes have learned from their Travel Mates is that there are many, many kind strangers in the world. Our Travel Mates travel through the "kindness of strangers" for the most part. The wonderful stories they collect in their journals, the post cards, and the souvenirs all tell the kids that there are many adults in the world who care about their education."
J. Moore, Winnetka, IL, USA

In the secondary area, examples of communication projects are wide ranging. Students in different countries may do similar experiments: for example, an experiment on local water quality. They then share the results – questioning the differences reported by the different countries. They may also take part in surveys for mathematics, history or geography and so on. Through these sorts of collaborative projects students develop their skills in using a wide range of ICT such as data logging, database, spreadsheet, desktop publishing, and e-mail and Internet in appropriate educational settings.

Further details of work using the Internet and e-mail in different subject areas are provided in two books with which the editors of *KeyBytes for Teachers* have been involved: *Teaching and Learning with ICT in the Secondary School* (Leask, M. and Pachler, N., 1999) and *Teaching and Learning with ICT in the Primary School* (Leask, M. and Meadows, J., 2000). Here we have just provided a taste of what is possible.

## LESSON PLANNING and CLASSROOM MANAGEMENT

### Effective lesson planning integrating ICT

Students will not necessarily learn just because they are using computers. Learning objectives (around aspects of learning such as concepts, attitudes, skills and knowledge) need to be defined for each lesson and should relate to learning outcomes related to the use of the technology as well as the curriculum area which provides the main focus for the lesson. The **Where in Oz/UK** project described earlier had clear objectives related to developing student skills and knowledge in geography and ICT. ICT like the old proverb about money, is a good servant but a bad master.

Margaret Cox (senior lecturer at Kings College, London) provides the following advice for the planning of lessons integrating ICT:

- tasks should be relevant to experiences at school or at home;
- students should be prepared for the task before they are assigned to computers;
- it is best if students do not sit at the computers while you are introducing the lesson;
- don't rely on the technology to run the lesson;
- don't expect the students to print out their work at the end of every lesson;
- intervene regularly to remind students of the educational purpose;
- draw students together at the end of the lesson to discuss what they have achieved. (adapted from Cox in Leask and Pachler, 1999, p. 30)

### Interactive worksheets

Interactive worksheets are being developed by teachers to integrate the resources on the Web into structured classroom activities.

Worksheets are constructed in the usual way but are made available to students on computers networked to the Internet as well as on paper as appropriate. In schools where practice is well developed banks of such worksheets are developed for each subject area and are held on the school's intranet. Where tasks are set which require students to access a particular web site, the address of the web site is included in the text of the worksheet which is open on the student's computer and the student clicks on the web site address to work with the Internet resource following the teachers' guidelines.

### Classroom management and access to computers

Where you do not have access to a whole classroom of computers, or enough computers for students to work in groups on tasks, there are other ways of providing Internet resources for the whole class. Interactive whiteboards, LCD projectors or large monitors linked to computers connected to the Internet can provide a way for the whole class to use the Internet.

Many of the ways in which teachers can use the Internet for projects only require one point of connection. For example, if e-mails are being sent to another school, they can be written on stand-alone computers, saved onto a disk and then taken to a computer which is connected up and sent. Where schools only have one point of connection it is often in the library and accessible to students for this sort of work.

One popular pattern of grouping of computers in primary schools is to have three or four points of connection in each classroom so that computers can be wheeled in from other classrooms when they are required allowing pupils to work together in groups, perhaps rotating access to the computers.

Where only dedicated computer rooms are available in schools, the access which individual teachers and students have to the technology may be too short in duration and too sporadic for 'deep learning' to take place. Decisions about the location and grouping of computers therefore need to take in account the ways in which teachers are likely to use them most effectively in teaching.

Health and safety issues must be considered by teachers when they are using computers with students. Work stations should be of an appropriate size and height and regulations regarding ways of working with computers should be checked with the school authorities. It is considered wise to ensure that if students' photographs and personal details are included on a school web site these should not be accessible to the general public.

## Teacher confidence

You may have valid concerns about hardware, software and communication links not being available at the time when you need them or not working at the time when you need them. Teachers need to be sure that lessons will run smoothly. Schools where staff are actively using Internet resources and using the potential of the Internet effectively usually have back-up plans in place to accommodate technical problems. Some of these have been mentioned earlier. For example, web sites can be downloaded onto a school's Intranet or an individual computer linked to the web. The sites are then available for you to use when you wish. The projects discussed above only require the computer for the sending and preparation of e-mails. Schools without an Internet connection have still taken part in such projects by using the resources of parents or local businesses in their community who do have connections.

Schools which are making most progress in this area are ones where staff support each other in ongoing learning about the technology. The rate of development of technology is such that ongoing learning is the norm. Michelle Selinger (Selinger, in Leask and Pachler, 1999) provides advice for teachers about how to manage the use of ICT with students when students may know more than the teacher:

> "Classroom dynamics with ICT alters considerably especially when teaching takes place in a computer room. There will be an increase in noise level and students may need to move freely around the classroom. It is also not always easy to be sure students are on-task, and you have to find ways of ascertaining this through questions and summing up sessions at the end of the lesson. You may well find yourself in the unusual position of knowing less than your students about hardware or software. There is no need to feel threatened by this situation; use it as an opportunity to increase your own knowledge, and to give students an opportunity to excel. Some software requires independent learning, but do not feel as though you are no longer teaching, your role as a mediator between the students and the machine is often crucial in developing their understanding. Questioning students about what they are doing, and why they are doing it in that way, demands that they have to articulate their understanding and in so doing can consolidate on their learning."

So the role of the teacher is more of a facilitator – working with the technology – than a giver of knowledge.

## USE OF THE INTERNET AND E-MAIL FOR YOUR OWN PROFESSIONAL DEVELOPMENT

Some of the ways in the Internet is being developed which can help your own professional development include:

- *Courses* – increasingly providers of courses for teachers are using the Internet in a variety of ways. Some courses are free, others you can only access through paying a fee.

- *Contacts* – through the partner finding activities described above, and through professional associations, you may be able to join a network of teachers interested in the same issues as yourself.

- *On-line Communities* – This term refers to places on the Web where teachers talk to each other about professional issues. You will find, for example, forums on the European Schoolnet site. Research communities in many countries can be located through the web site of the British Educational Research Association (**http://www/bera.ac.uk**) – click on the 'web links' button on the front page.

- *Access to resources from experts* – this was discussed at the beginning of this unit. You may find it easier to keep up to date in your subject area through consulting the web sites of organisations working in areas related to your specialist interest.

- *Government documentation* – many governments now put educational materials on the web. One way through to the government networks in Europe is to click on the partner networks button on the European Schoolnet site. This provides a page linking the networks of 18 European countries. Government sponsored sites of particular interest to UK teachers include the National Grid For Learning (NGFL) on **http://www.ngfl.gov.uk/** and the Commonwealth Electronic Network of Schools **http://www.col.org/cense/** (which provides links to 54 Commonwealth countries). The sites of the Department for Education and Employment (DFEE), **http://www.dfee.gov.uk/**;Teacher Training Agency, **http://www.teach-tta.gov.uk/** and OFSTED **http://www.ofsted.gov.uk/** all provide documentation which teachers may find useful.

The last unit in the book (pages 173–181) is a self assessment unit to help you plan your further professional development.

## SUMMARY SUMMARY SUMMARY SUMMARY SUMMARY

- The Internet provides resources as well as a means for communication.
- The quality of material found on the Internet has to be checked for reliability.
- Lesson planning which identifies specific objectives to be achieved through using the e-mail and Internet technology is essential – the technology is only useful for certain educational purposes. It does not replace the teacher.
- Many innovative Internet-based projects require students to have access to only one point of connection to the Internet – for the sending and receiving of e-mails.
- An increasing variety of continuing professional development opportunities are available through the Web.

Now try the following tasks:

**TASKS**

1. Explore the projects listed on the European Schoolnet and British Council Montage sites and consider what sort of project your own pupils might find educationally useful and enjoyable. Our advice is to start with a small project running over a short time, e.g. a survey of leisure habits; food choices; sporting activities; aspects of the local environment, etc, to develop your skills in managing such projects.

2. Explore what the Internet has to offer you for your own professional development. Talk to colleagues about what they find useful; ask your professional associations and colleagues in teacher training organisations.

### References

[1] Leafe, D., *Managing Curriculum Projects with ICT*, in Leask, M. and Meadows, J., *Teaching and Learning with ICT in the Primary School*, Routledge, London, 2000.

[2] Selinger, M., *ICT and Classroom Management*, in Leask, M. and Pachler, N., *Teaching and Learning with ICT in the Secondary School*, Routledge, London, 2000.

# KeyBytes Final Test

Now you're almost at the end of your course. After the *KeyBytes Final Test* there is a unit that gives you the opportunity to plan your further development.

You've practised a great many things and will have developed good basic ICT skills. You are ready to move out of the 'controlled environment' of *KeyBytes* and use a whole range of different programs.

Remember, you can always refer to your *KeyBytes* program and you won't ever go far wrong!

You also know about the role of ICT in society – and have been introduced to a range of educational applications. You now appreciate why it can be a good idea to use touch screens, databases, spreadsheets, DTP, the Internet, etc.

Issues relating to the *quality of information* and the design of information have been raised.

You now have the opportunity to have your knowledge and understanding examined by answering the 40 questions in the *Keybytes Final Test*.

The test is linked to the program units you have completed.

Once you finish the test *KeyBytes* will calculate your final result and print out your Diploma.

**Good luck!**

# Self Assessment to Create Your Personal Action Plan

## INTRODUCTION

At any stage in the *KeyBytes* programme, you might wish to evaluate your growing expertise in ICT. This process will allow you to note relevant information in a systematic way, which in turn will help to inform the subsequent choices and decisions you take about your professional development. Your self assessment using this chapter can be formative, in that the analysis of your current skills and expertise can be used to support an action plan to address areas of need. It can also be summative, in that the assessment can be used as a summary of your ICT status at the end of your *KeyBytes* work.

### Objectives

The purpose of this unit is to enable you to identify the strengths and weakness in your information technology skills. It also allows you to assess your use of ICT in the classroom. The assessment can be used as the basis for a personal action plan for your professional development in this area. The information can also be used to discuss with others the management and organisational changes which will help you to assimilate ICT into your classroom practice.

By the end of this chapter you should have:

- completed a self assessment process.
- formulated a personal action plan based on this assessment.
- identified key factors on which discussion of your professional development in ICT might be based.

## BACKGROUND

Three ways of evaluating your opportunities to use ICT are included in this chapter. Each addresses a different aspect of competence. You may wish to read through all the tables to select which is appropriate for your present purposes. Guidelines are included after each table, to enable you to translate your analysis into an action plan or discussion document. Below are summaries of the purposes of each assessment.

## Self Assessment

### Evaluation 1: Your present school context

This provides an overview of the context for your inclusion of ICT in your classroom practice. It asks you to consider details of the computer provision you have at home and at school, and then goes on to look at some aspects of training.

### Evaluation 2: Your history and experience

This provides a structure for reflection on factors which have been found to influence the way teachers use ICT. Looking at such key issues helps to provide information which can then be used to make decisions about what changes are desirable or possible.

### Evaluation 3: Your teaching with ICT

Based on the UK Teacher Training Agency's requirements for new teachers, this evaluation concerns the use of ICT for effective teaching and assessment. The questions deal with such issues as the appropriate use of ICT, planning for ICT use, and organisation of resources. Consideration of these issues will help you to identify areas where you are more or less confident, so that you can make decisions about what course of action to take.

---

You can fill in the evaluation tables on screen and print them out as a record of your self assessment

---

Self Assessment

## Table A: Evaluation 1: Your present school context

Answer the questions below by choosing the box which most closely matches your situation.

| | Question | Yes | No |
|---|---|---|---|
| A | **Personal computer: at home** | | |
| | Do you have access to a computer? | | |
| | If yes, is it shared with other people? | | |
| | If yes, do you use it for work purposes? | | |
| | If yes, do you use e-mail regularly at home? | | |
| | Do you use the Internet regularly at home? | | |
| | Do you regularly have online contact with other teachers? | | |
| | Do you use electronic conferencing/chat/bulletin boards? | | |
| | If no, do you plan to get a computer? | | |
| | What would encourage you to do so? | | |
| | Do you think that the use of computers with students sometimes lacks a clear educational purpose? | | |
| | Do you consider computers to be more useful to you out of the classroom? | | |
| | Have you read or heard of research evidence focused on the educational value of ICT? | | |
| B | **Personal computer: at school** | | |
| | Do you have a computer for your sole use? | | |
| | Do you have accessible technical support? | | |
| | Do you have a personal e-mail address? | | |
| | Do you use e-mail frequently (most days)? | | |
| | Is time allocated for your computer use? | | |
| C | **School computer room** | | |
| | Do you have access to a computer room? | | |
| | Is your access regularly timetabled? | | |
| | Do you have accessible technical support? | | |
| | Do you have other adult support? | | |
| | Are there 3 or more different makes of computer? | | |
| | Are the computers more than 3 years old? | | |
| | Are they networked to one another? | | |
| | Do you include this facility in your planning? | | |
| | Have you had training to use these computers in the last year? | | |

## Self Assessment

|   |   | Yes | No |
|---|---|---|---|
|   | **School computer room (cont.)** |   |   |
|   | Do you find visits to the computer room productive, or educationally effective? |   |   |
|   | Are the computers linked to the Internet? |   |   |
|   | Do students have (and use) e-mail addresses? |   |   |
|   | Do you plan and undertake Internet projects? |   |   |
|   | Do you use electronic conferencing/chat/bulletin boards at work? |   |   |
|   | Do you regularly have online contact with other teachers at work? |   |   |
| D | **School computers: Classroom** |   |   |
|   | Do you have computer(s) in your classroom? |   |   |
|   | Are they less than 3 years old? |   |   |
|   | Do you have accessible technical support? |   |   |
|   | Are computers linked to the Internet? |   |   |
|   | Are they networked within the school? |   |   |
|   | Do you include this facility in your planning? |   |   |
|   | Do you find its use educationally effective? |   |   |
|   | Does it create problems sometimes? |   |   |
|   | Have you had training to use classroom computers within the last year? |   |   |
| E | **Professional development** |   |   |
|   | Is ICT training a first priority for your professional development? |   |   |
|   | Do you feel that your current ICT skills and understanding are adequate to support your teaching using ICT? |   |   |
|   | Do you feel that you have adequate equipment to support the ICT work you wish to do with your students? |   |   |
|   | Do you feel that you receive adequate technical support? |   |   |
|   | Do you feel that you receive adequate support in your planning for use of ICT? |   |   |
|   | Do you have time allocated to you in which you can plan, prepare or practise using ICT? |   |   |

Consider the questions you have answered.

Choose *five factors* which you think would make most difference to your classroom use of ICT. List them in order with the most important first. Where you have answered 'No' to a question, consider whether there are actions which you might take to improve the situation.

## WHAT NEXT?

Consider your answers to each of the sections in Table A.

*Home computer*: The ownership of a home computer has been found to help teachers to become more fluent users of ICT. Computer skills learned at home in a (slightly!) more relaxed environment can be used in school. Some schools and local or regional authorities organise leasing schemes, whilst others provide interest free loans: what is available for you? Perhaps it is possible to take a school computer home to use. Once you own a computer, you may find various companies offer free Internet access.

*Personal computer at School*: The provision of personal computers for teachers at work is unusual, and you may feel unnecessary. Would it help? To what purposes would you put a computer of your own at school?

*School computer room*: School hardware can make a huge difference to the way you use ICT. Ageing, unmatched machines with no technical back up have limited use. It may be useful to consider what changes can be made, within the school's financial constraints.

*Classroom computers*: Do you feel that yours are used effectively? What changes could be made in order to maximise their use? How are other classroom computers used within your school?

*Professional development*: ICT may not be your first priority for professional development. There may be conflicting demands. It is worth taking a longer view and trying to work out when further training would be most appropriate for you. Meanwhile, informal learning is always possible, especially if you can collaborate with colleagues. For this to happen, time has to be organised.

Organise a meeting with the ICT Co-ordinator of your school, or the member of staff in charge of professional development. Discuss what would help you improve your practice now and decide on a plan in order to work towards future changes. You may wish to complete the following two self-analysis questionnaires before having this meeting.

## Self Assessment

## Table B: Evaluation 2: Your history and experience

Answer the questions below analysing your history and experience.

|  | Your history and experience |
|---|---|
| **A.** What training have you received for the computers and other ICT that is available in your school or classroom? How recent was the training? Have you been able to incorporate your new learning into your practice? If not, why? If yes, will you continue to use what you have learnt, or is it not relevant to your usual classroom practice? |  |
| **B.** What do you consider to be the most effective uses of classroom or school computers that you have developed and used with students? Have you had chance to share these with other teachers at your school? |  |
| **C.** What skills or experience of ICT do you have that you feel are under-used in your teaching? What factors prevent you using these skills? |  |
| **D.** What are the main difficulties when using your school's computers? Are these specific problems with the machines, or are there management or organisational problems? |  |
| **E.** Is ICT a real priority for you? If yes, which aspect of your own ICT skills or understanding do you wish to address? If no, what are the competing priorities? |  |
| **F.** Do you have a friend, a relative or a colleague who regularly helps you with ICT? Are there others around who can help you? Do you help others with ICT? |  |
| **G.** In an ideal world, what would be necessary in order to help you assimilate ICT more fully into your classroom practice; or do you think that increased use is unnecessary? |  |

## WHAT NEXT?

Consider your answers to each of the sections in Table B. Use what you have recorded to identify the barriers which make it difficult for you to move ahead with your ICT development.

Decide: what are your priorities for the coming year? The following list provides a framework for this analysis. Make notes specifying the action you wish to take and how you might manage conflicting priorities.

A: Training

B: Collaborative experience and sharing ICT expertise

C: Developing skills and their application

D: Knowledge about hardware and software

E: Reliable technical support

F: 'Wish list'

## Self Assessment

## Table C: Evaluation 3: Your teaching with ICT

Read the statements and allocate yourself to one of the categories.

*I use Information and Communication Technology with students:*

| Statement | Adept | Working knowledge | Beginner |
|---|---|---|---|
| To store and retrieve information | | | |
| To process and present work | | | |
| For models and simulations | | | |
| Directly linked to teaching and learning objectives | | | |
| To assess and record student progress | | | |
| To judge progress in curriculum areas when ICT is used | | | |
| Appropriately differentiated for individual students | | | |
| Avoiding unnecessary use | | | |
| Stressing the importance of content over presentation | | | |
| Structuring the task to avoid students wasting time | | | |
| With high expectations for all students | | | |
| With individuals, pairs, groups and whole classes | | | |
| With due consideration of health and safety | | | |
| Ensuring ICT supports rather than dominates work | | | |
| To support students with Special Educational Needs | | | |
| To support students with English as a second or other language | | | |
| Reviewing new applications for suitability and educational effectiveness | | | |
| Reviewing available software for suitability and educational effectiveness | | | |
| Using and explaining ICT terminology | | | |
| Modelling good practice with equipment | | | |
| Discussing ICT use with students | | | |
| Ensuring students fully reference their work | | | |
| Recognising individual achievement in group work | | | |
| Assessing learning rather than presentation | | | |
| Ensuring opportunities to demonstrate achievement | | | |
| To consolidate literacy | | | |
| To consolidate numeracy | | | |
| Creatively, to explore and experiment | | | |

## WHAT NEXT?

Look at the pattern of your responses to the questions in Table C.

Where you have categorised yourself as 'Adept', can you offer to provide support or training for others?

Where you have categorised yourself as having a 'Working knowledge', identify a colleague at a similar level for discussion and investigation of new directions.

Where you have categorised yourself as 'Beginner', consider your priorities for your professional development over the next year.

If you have not already planned to do so, organise a meeting with your ICT Co-ordinator to discuss your ideas, and to draw up a realistic Action Plan to guide your progress. Identify a colleague with similar priorities and arrange to discuss new ideas together in order to consolidate learning. Choose one area of the curriculum in which you feel that ICT could enhance the learning of your students, and use that as a context for your own professional development.

## GOODBYE ...

The editorial team and the publisher of *KeyBytes* all hope that you enjoyed this learning process. We wish you the very best in your continuing professional development.

If you have any questions please send them to:

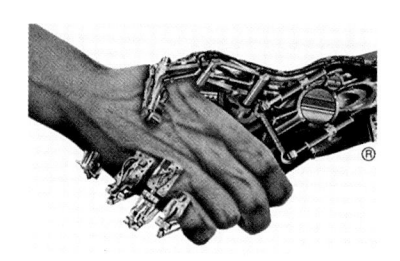

The Publisher
Summerfield Publishing Ltd
PO Box 16
Evesham
WR11 6WN
Great Britain
e-mail: info@keybytes.co.uk

# Index

access rights 144, 147–8
addresses 149, 156
artificial intelligence 129–30
attachments, e-mail 144, 150

back-up 3, 25, 65
barcodes 136, 139
binary code 23, 40

CAD 99, 103–6
calculations 82–5
CAM 99, 103–4, 105–6
cameras 36–7, 45, 124–5
cars 105, 128, 137
  *see also* roads
CD-ROMs 3, 25–6, 139, 155
cells, spreadsheet 77, 78–9, 82–3
chips *see* memory; processors
clipart 99, 102–3
columns, spreadsheet 78–9, 85
communications 143–60, 162–3
computer-controlled machines 121–31
control 126–8
copying 70, 82–3
cursors 4–5, 9, 11, 13–14, 66
cutting text 70

data 20, 21, 89
  storage *see* disks
databases 89–97
data loggers 48, 123, 136
deleting 12, 66, 70
design 103–6, 110–17
desktop publishing (DTP) 108–9,
  117–18
digital devices 23, 40, 44–5
disks 3, 23–6, 65, 139, 155
dot-matrix printers 41
downloading 40, 144, 156
drawings *see* graphics
DTP (desktop publishing) 108–9,
  117–18
DVD drives 26

e-mail 28, 148–50, 161–71

fax 144, 152
fields, database 89, 90–2
file formats 99, 101
floppy disks 3, 23–4, 65
flow charts 125, 134, 141
folders in windows 52–3, 60
fonts 69, 114–15
formulas 82–5
frames, DTP 109, 117–18
function keys 9, 14

graphical user interfaces (GUI) 52
graphics (drawings) 51, 73, 98–107
  in DTP 115–17, 118, 119
graphs in spreadsheets 86
GUI (graphical user interfaces) 52

hard disks 24–5
hardware 2–4, 20–30, 46
help 10, 58–9
highlighting text 68
hyperlinks 118–19, 144

importing 73, 109
industry, computer-control in 121–31
inkjet printers 42, 43
input 9, 31, 44–6
  *see also* keyboards; mice
interactive whiteboards 36, 132, 138
interactive worksheets 168
interfaces 51, 52
Internet 40, 74, 139–40, 148, 149–50
  in teaching 161–71
intranets 110, 153–4

joysticks 45

keyboards 3, 4–5, 9–16, 48

LANs (local area networks) 145
laser printers 41–2
layout, spreadsheet 77, 80–1
LCD (liquid crystal display) 33, 35
legislation 95, 103
libraries 138–9
liquid crystal display (LCD) 33, 35
local area networks (LANs) 145
logging on 144

manufacturing 103–6
measurement 126–8
megabytes 22, 23
memory 22–3
mice 3, 5–6, 13, 57
microphones 47
modelling 77, 85–6
modems 46, 151
monitors (screens) 2, 31–9
multimedia 108, 109, 110, 119
music keyboards 48

networks 25, 65, 145–8, 151–2
  *see also* Internet; intranets

offensive material 158
opening files and folders 52–3, 72
output 31, 32, 41–3, 46
  *see also* printers; screens

passwords vi–x
pasting 70
peripherals 40–50
pixels 33–4
plotters 43
police, computer use by 136–7
power 26, 35
printers and printing 41–2, 65
processors 2, 21–2
programs 2, 4, 21, 28, 46–7

for computer-control 123–6
for graphics 99–103
projection systems 35–6
projects 161–7
publishing 108–20

RAM (Random Access Memory) 22
Read Only Memory (ROM) 22
records, database 90, 91–2
remote access 144, 151–2
resolution 33–4
resources 161–7
roads 129–30, 133–4
  *see also* cars
robots 122–4, 125–7, 129–30
ROM (Read Only Memory) 22
rows, spreadsheet 78–9, 85

saving 65, 101
scanning 44, 103
screens 2, 31–9
searching 72, 91–2, 155, 157
security checks 132, 135, 136
selecting 68
self-assessment 173–81
sensors 27, 122
servers 25, 145
shopping, Internet 157–9
shortcuts 56, 60, 70
software *see* programs
sorting, database 89, 91–2
speakers 3, 27, 47
spreadsheets 76–88
starting programs in windows 52–3
surfing the net 144, 157–9

teaching 105–6, 137–40, 152, 180–1
  Internet in 139–40, 161–71
templates, DTP 110, 117–18
touch screens 34–5
toys and games 140
typing 17–19

VDU screens 2, 31–9
video conferencing 36–7, 138, 162–3
virtual reality 37
viruses 28, 47, 156
voice messages 144, 152

WANs (wide area networks) 145–6,
  151–2
Web, World Wide 144, 155–9
  *see also* Internet
what if problems 85–6
whiteboards 36, 132, 138
wide area networks (WANs) 145–6,
  151–2
Windows 51–62
word processing 63–75

182

# Acknowledgements

The Publishers are grateful to the following for permission to reproduce photographs and other copyright materials in this book:

Alan Clarke/Caltek Ltd – page 128 (lower)
Benelux Press – page 146
Chriet Titulaar Produckties – pages 37 (upper) and 123
*Daily Telegraph* – page 113
Hewlett Packard – pages 42 (lower right) and 44 (lower)
KLM – page 37 (lower)
Martyn Chillmaid – page 45
*Mizz* magazine – pages 111 and 116
Postercraft, Cheltenham – page 43 (lower)
Promethean Ltd – page 36 (upper)
Rover Group Ltd – page 121
Sam Ogden/SPL – page 129
Science and Society Picture Library – page 6
Sony – page 138
The Rijksmuseum, Amsterdam – page 63
*The Sun* – page 112
Trip/H Rogers – page 36 (lower)

Thanks also to Evesham Micros for various photographs of computer equipment and to Robert Hale of Longdon Hill Nursery for help with the greenhouse section.

Every effort has been made to acknowledge copyright holders. We apologise if any have been overlooked and will be pleased to rectify this at the earliest opportunity.